JUNIOR SCHOOL ATLAS

LIST OF CONTENTS

Royal Geographical Society
with IBG

Advancing geography
and geographical learning

Philip's World Atlases are published in association with The Royal Geographical Society (with The Institute of British Geographers).

The Society was founded in 1830 and given a Royal Charter in 1859 for 'the advancement of geographical science'. Today it is a leading world centre for geographical learning – supporting education, teaching, research and expeditions, and promoting public understanding of the subject.

Further information about the Society and how to join may be found on its website at: **www.rgs.org**

Published in Great Britain by Philip's,
a division of Octopus Publishing Group Limited
(www.octopusbooks.co.uk)
Carmelite House, 50 Victoria Embankment,
London EC4Y 0DZ
An Hachette UK Company (www.hachette.co.uk)

Cartography by Philip's

© 2021 Philip's
First published 1993
Second edition 1997
Third edition 1999
Fourth edition 2003
Fifth edition 2006
Sixth edition 2008
Seventh edition 2011
Eighth edition 2014
Ninth edition 2015
Tenth edition 2019
Eleventh edition 2021

A CIP catalogue record for this book is available from the British Library.

ISBN 978-1-84907-579-4 (HARDBACK EDITION)
ISBN 978-1-84907-580-0 (PAPERBACK EDITION)

Printed in Dubai

Details of other Philip's titles and services can be found on our website at: **www.philips-maps.co.uk**

Using this atlas

How to use this atlas

The atlas is in five colour coded sections. These are shown on the **List of contents** on the page opposite.

There are two ways to find information in this atlas.

- Firstly, if you are looking for a particular topic, look for it on the **List of contents** on the page opposite or on the **Subject list** on this page. For example, maps showing Energy resources can be found on pages 15 and 41.

- Secondly, if you are looking for a particular place or feature, look for the name of the place in the **Index of place names** on pages 64–65. You can refer to page 63 **Finding places** to help you find the place on the map. If you know roughly where a particular name occurs, you can use the **Key map of the continents** below or the **List of contents** to find the map page number and then look for it on the map.

Subject list

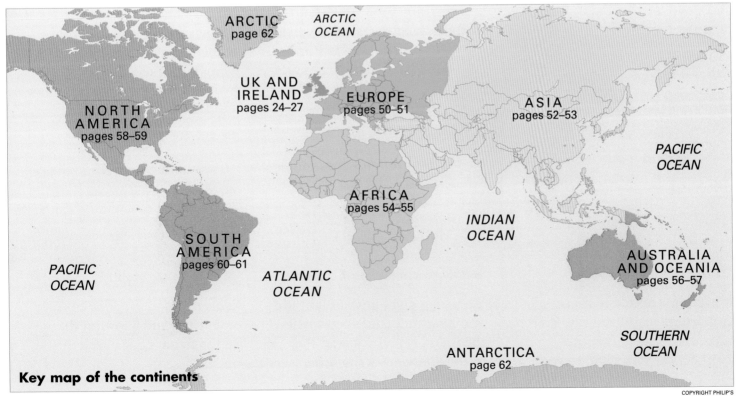

Key map of the continents

ARCTIC page 62 — ARCTIC OCEAN

UK AND IRELAND pages 24–27

EUROPE pages 50–51

ASIA pages 52–53

NORTH AMERICA pages 58–59

PACIFIC OCEAN

AFRICA pages 54–55

INDIAN OCEAN

SOUTH AMERICA pages 60–61

PACIFIC OCEAN

ATLANTIC OCEAN

AUSTRALIA AND OCEANIA pages 56–57

ANTARCTICA page 62

SOUTHERN OCEAN

What is a map?

These small maps explain the meaning of some of the lines and colours on the atlas maps.

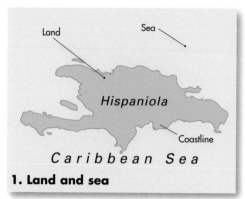

1. Land and sea

This is how an island is shown on a map. The land is coloured green and the sea is blue. The coastline is a blue line.

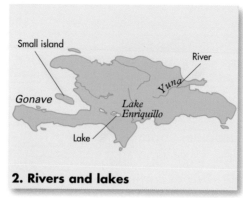

2. Rivers and lakes

There are some lakes on the island and rivers that flow down to the sea.

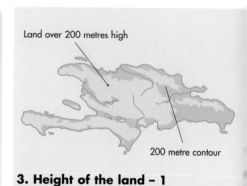

3. Height of the land – 1

This map shows the land over 200 metres high in a lighter colour. The height of the land is shown by contour lines and layer colours.

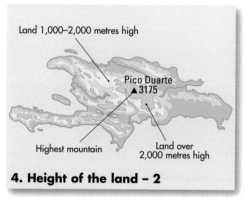

4. Height of the land – 2

This map shows more contour lines and layer colours. It shows that the highest mountain is in the centre of the island and that it is over 3,000 metres high.

5. Countries

This is a way of showing different information about the island. It shows that the island is divided into two countries. They are separated by a country boundary.

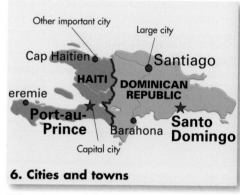

6. Cities and towns

There are cities and towns on the island. The two capital cities are shown with a special symbol. Other large or important cities are shown by a red circle.

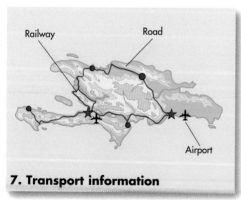

7. Transport information

This map shows the most important roads, railways and airports. Transport routes connect the cities and towns.

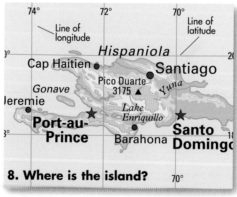

8. Where is the island?

This map gives lines of latitude and longitude and shows where the island is in the world. Page 59 in the atlas shows the same island on a map at a different scale.

9. A complete map

This map is using the country colouring and showing the letter-figure codes used in the index.

2

Map information

Symbols

Page 17

A map symbol shows the position of something – for example, circles for towns or an aeroplane for an airport.

Page 46

On some maps a dot or a symbol stands for a large number – for example, 500,000 people or cities with over 10 million people.

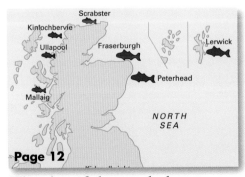
Page 12

The size of the symbol can be bigger or smaller, to show different numbers. The symbol here shows fishing ports in the UK.

Colours

Page 51

Colours are used on some maps so that separate areas, such as countries, as in this map, can be seen clearly.

Page 8

On other maps, areas that are the same in some way have the same colour to show patterns. This map shows rainfall.

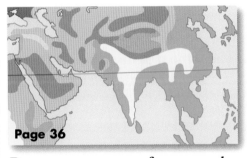
Page 36

Patterns on maps often spread across country borders. This map shows different types of vegetation in the world.

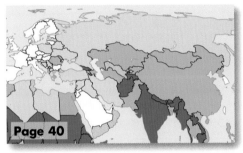
Page 40

Colours that are lighter or darker are used on some maps to show less or more of something. This map shows farming.

Graphs and charts

Graphs and charts are used to give more information about subjects shown on the maps. A graph shows how something changes over time.

This graph shows the rainfall for each month in a year as a blue bar that can be measured on the scale at the side of the graph.

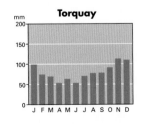

Page 8

This diagram is called a pie-chart. It shows how you can divide a total into its parts. It shows where the food eaten in the UK comes from.

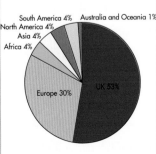

Page 12

This is a bar-chart. It is another way of showing a total divided into parts.

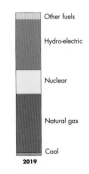

Page 15

Scale

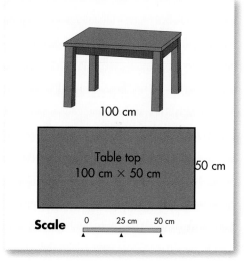

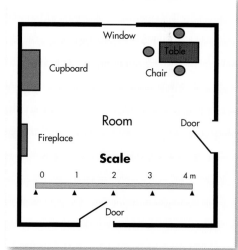

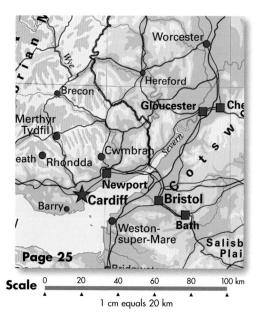

This is a drawing of the top of a table, looking down on it. It is 100 cm long and 50 cm wide. The drawing measures 4 × 2 cm. It is drawn to scale: 1 cm on the drawing equals 25 cm on the table.

This is a plan of a room looking down from above. 1 cm on the plan equals 1 metre in the room. The same table is shown, but now at a smaller scale. Use the scale bar to find the measurements of other parts of the room.

This is an even smaller scale plan that shows the table in a room, inside a house. 1 cm on the plan equals 4 metres in the house. We can also call this a large scale map.

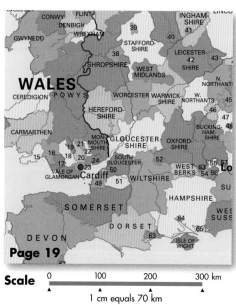

Scale bars

This distance represents 1 mile

This distance represents 1 kilometre

These examples of scale bars are at the scale of 1 cm equals 0.5 km

Signposts still have miles on them. 1 mile = 1.6 km, or 10 miles is the same as 16 kilometres.
On the maps of the UK and Ireland and the continents kilometre scale

bars are used. On the maps of the continents, where you cannot see the UK and Ireland, a small map is shown to give you some idea of size and scale.

UK & IRELAND
On same scale

Direction

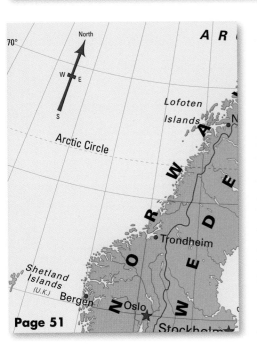

Page 51

The Cardinal Points

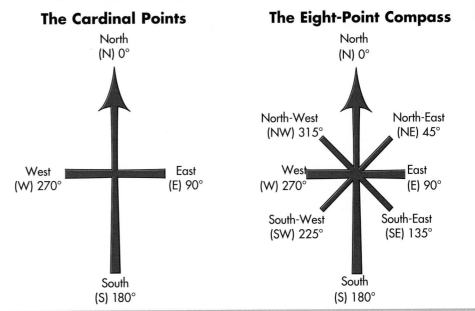

The Eight-Point Compass

North (N) 0°

West (W) 270°   East (E) 90°

South (S) 180°

North (N) 0°

North-West (NW) 315°   North-East (NE) 45°

West (W) 270°   East (E) 90°

South-West (SW) 225°   South-East (SE) 135°

South (S) 180°

Many of the maps in this atlas have a North Point showing the direction of north. It points in the same direction as the lines of longitude. The four main directions shown are called the cardinal points.

Direction is measured in degrees. This diagram shows the degree numbers for each cardinal point. The direction is measured clockwise from north. The diagram on the right shows all the points of the compass and the divisions between the cardinal points. For example, between north and east there is north-east, between south and west is south-west. You can work out the cardinal points at your home by looking for the sun rising in the east and setting in the west.

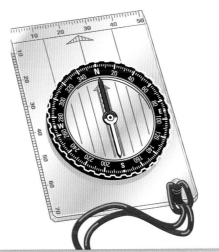

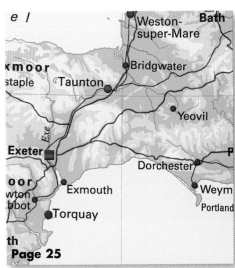

Page 25

The Earth has a spot near the North Pole that is called the Magnetic Pole. If a piece of metal that was magnetized at one end was left to float, then the magnetized tip would point to the North Magnetic Pole.

The needle of a compass is magnetized and it always points north. If you know where you are and want to go to another place, you can measure your direction from a map and use a compass to guide you.

North is at the top of this map. Look at the points of the compass on the diagram above and the positions of places on the map. Taunton is north-east of Exeter and Dorchester is south-east of Taunton.

Rocks, mountains and rivers

Rocks

This map shows the different types of rock in Great Britain and Ireland.

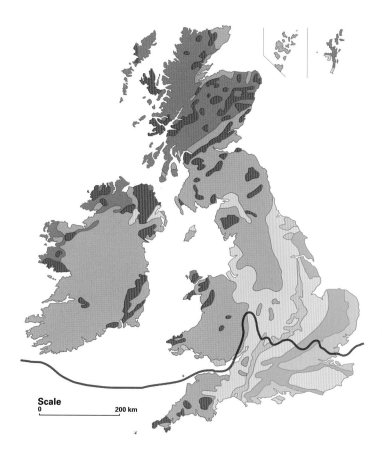

Scale
0   200 km

Type of rock

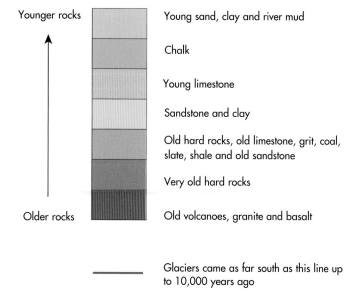

Younger rocks

	Young sand, clay and river mud
	Chalk
	Young limestone
	Sandstone and clay
	Old hard rocks, old limestone, grit, coal, slate, shale and old sandstone
	Very old hard rocks
	Old volcanoes, granite and basalt

Older rocks

———— Glaciers came as far south as this line up to 10,000 years ago

Longest rivers
(length in kilometres)

1. Shannon 370
2. Severn 354
3. Thames 335
4. Trent 297
5. Aire 259
6. Great Ouse 230
7. Wye 215
8. Tay 188
9. Nene 161
10. Clyde 158

The longest river in Northern Ireland is the River Bann (129 kilometres). The longest river completely in Wales is the Tywi (109 kilometres).

Largest lakes
(area in square kilometres)

1. Lough Neagh 382
2. Lough Corrib 168
3. Lough Derg 120
4. Lower Lough Erne 105
5. Loch Lomond 71
6. Loch Ness 57

The largest lake in England is Windermere (15 square kilometres). The largest lake in Wales is Llyn Vyrnwy (8 square kilometres).

Largest islands
(area in square kilometres)

1. Great Britain 229,880
2. Ireland 84,400
3. Lewis and Harris 2,225
4. Skye 1,666
5. Shetland (Mainland) 967
6. Mull 899
7. Anglesey 714
8. Islay 615
9. Isle of Man 572
10. Isle of Wight 381

Highest mountains
(height in metres)

In Scotland:
  Ben Nevis 1,345
In Wales:
  Snowdon 1,085
In Ireland:
  Carrauntoohill 1,041
In England:
  Scafell Pike 978
In Northern Ireland:
  Slieve Donard 852

Scale
0   200 km

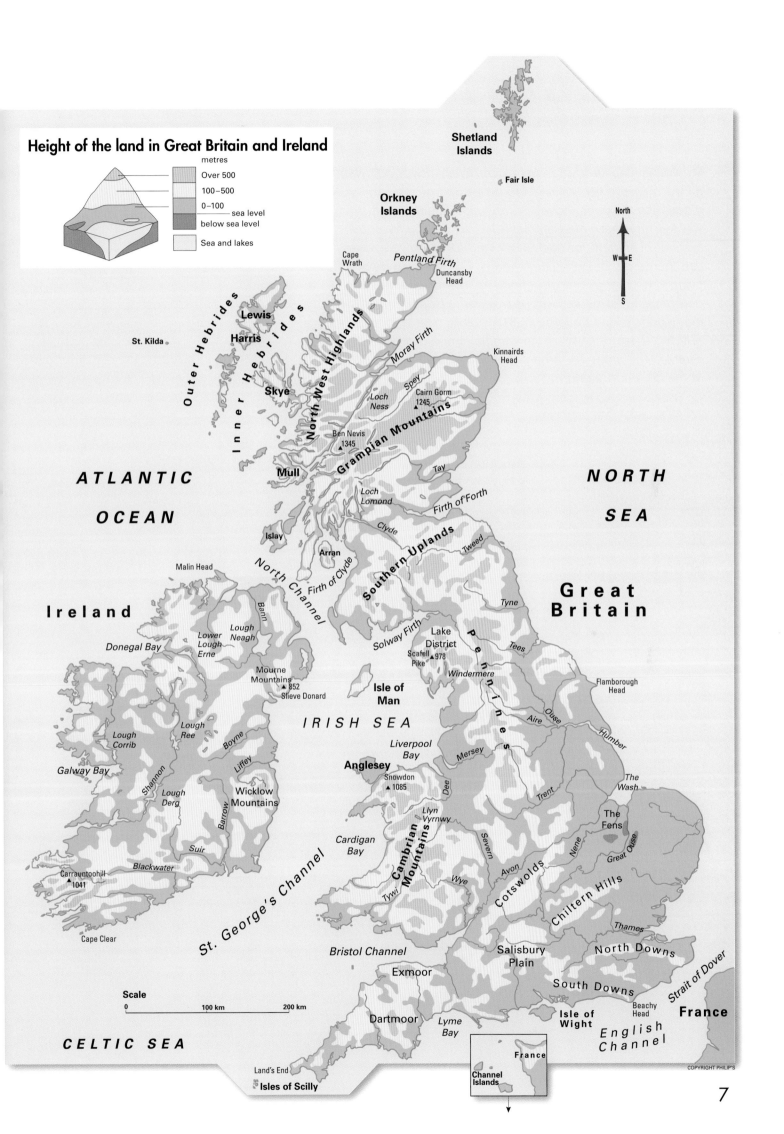

Height of the land in Great Britain and Ireland

metres
- Over 500
- 100–500
- 0–100 — sea level
- below sea level
- Sea and lakes

North
W–E
S

Shetland Islands

Fair Isle

Orkney Islands

Cape Wrath
Pentland Firth
Duncansby Head

Outer Hebrides

Lewis

Harris

St. Kilda

Inner Hebrides

Skye

North West Highlands

Moray Firth

Kinnairds Head

Loch Ness

Spey

Cairn Gorm 1245 ▲

Grampian Mountains

Ben Nevis 1345 ▲

Mull

Tay

ATLANTIC

OCEAN

Loch Lomond

Firth of Forth

Islay

Clyde

Arran

Firth of Clyde

N O R T H

S E A

Tweed

Southern Uplands

Malin Head

North Channel

Tyne

**G r e a t
B r i t a i n**

Ireland

Bann

Lough Neagh

Lower Lough Erne

Solway Firth

Lake District
Scafell Pike ▲ 978

Pennines

Tees

Donegal Bay

Mourne Mountains
▲ 852
Slieve Donard

Isle of Man

Windermere

Flamborough Head

Lough Ree

Boyne

IRISH SEA

Aire

Ouse

Humber

Lough Corrib

Lough

Liffey

Liverpool Bay

Mersey

Galway Bay

Shannon

Lough Derg

Anglesey

The Wash

Snowdon ▲ 1085

Dee

Trent

The Fens

Barrow

Wicklow Mountains

Llyn Vyrnwy

Cambrian Mountains

Nene

Great Ouse

Suir

Blackwater

Cardigan Bay

Cotswolds

Chiltern Hills

Carrauntoohill ▲ 1041

Severn

Avon

Tywi

Wye

Thames

Cape Clear

St. George's Channel

Bristol Channel

Salisbury Plain

North Downs

Scale
0   100 km   200 km

Exmoor

South Downs

Beachy Head

France

CELTIC SEA

Dartmoor

Lyme Bay

Isle of Wight

English Channel

Strait of Dover

Land's End

Isles of Scilly

France

Channel Islands

COPYRIGHT PHILIP'S

7

Weather and climate

Rainfall is measured at many places every day. Each year, all the measurements are put together and graphs are made, like the ones shown on this page. Experts in the weather use these measurements to find out the average amount of rainfall for each place and for each year. They can then show this on climate maps, like the map below. Graphs and maps are also made for average temperatures and other types of weather (see opposite page). These help the experts to see patterns in the weather over a long period of time. These patterns in the weather show a country's climate. The maps on these pages show you the climate of the UK and Ireland.

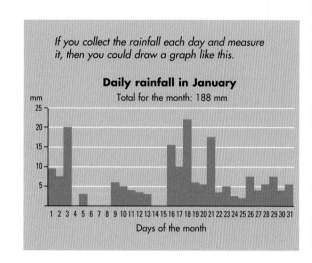

If you collect the rainfall each day and measure it, then you could draw a graph like this.

Daily rainfall in January
Total for the month: 188 mm

Days of the month

Rainfall

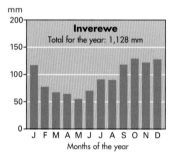

Inverewe
Total for the year: 1,128 mm
Months of the year

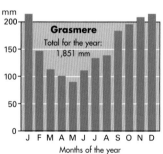

Grasmere
Total for the year: 1,851 mm
Months of the year

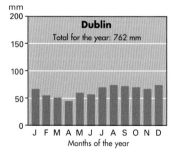

Dublin
Total for the year: 762 mm
Months of the year

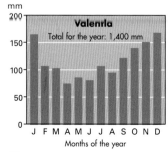

Valentia
Total for the year: 1,400 mm
Months of the year

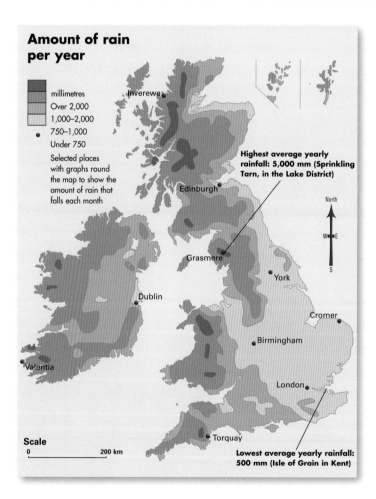

Amount of rain per year

millimetres
Over 2,000
1,000–2,000
750–1,000
Under 750

Selected places with graphs round the map to show the amount of rain that falls each month

Inverewe

Edinburgh

Highest average yearly rainfall: 5,000 mm (Sprinkling Tarn, in the Lake District)

Grasmere

York

Dublin

Cromer

Birmingham

Valentia

London

Torquay

Lowest average yearly rainfall: 500 mm (Isle of Grain in Kent)

North
W—E
S

Scale
0   200 km

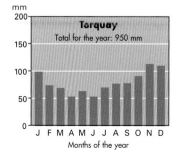

Torquay
Total for the year: 950 mm
Months of the year

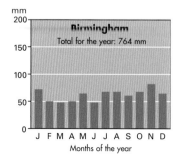

Birmingham
Total for the year: 764 mm
Months of the year

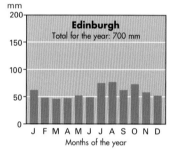

Edinburgh
Total for the year: 700 mm
Months of the year

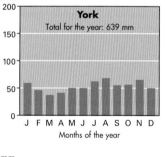

York
Total for the year: 639 mm
Months of the year

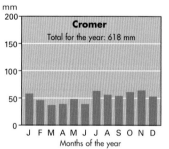

Cromer
Total for the year: 618 mm
Months of the year

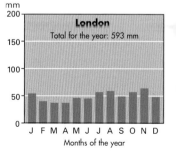

London
Total for the year: 593 mm
Months of the year

Wind

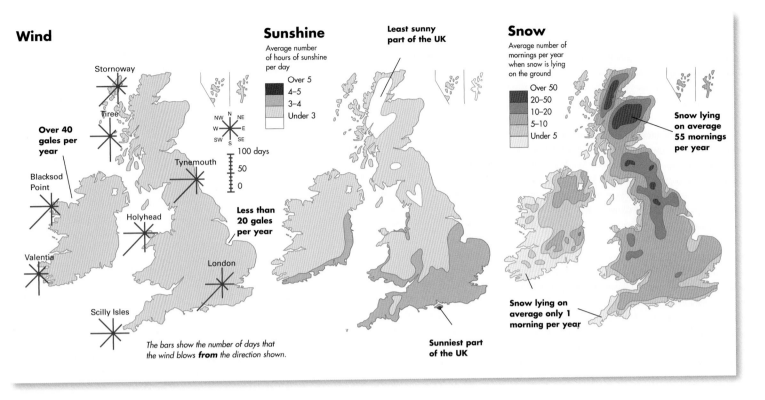

Stornoway

Tiree

Over 40 gales per year

Blacksod Point

Tynemouth

Holyhead

Valentia

London

Less than 20 gales per year

Scilly Isles

*The bars show the number of days that the wind blows **from** the direction shown.*

Sunshine

Average number of hours of sunshine per day

- Over 5
- 4–5
- 3–4
- Under 3

NW N NE
W E
SW S SE

100 days
50
0

Least sunny part of the UK

Sunniest part of the UK

Snow

Average number of mornings per year when snow is lying on the ground

- Over 50
- 20–50
- 10–20
- 5–10
- Under 5

Snow lying on average 55 mornings per year

Snow lying on average only 1 morning per year

Temperature

Birmingham
°C
Average temperature for year: 10°C
J F M A M J J A S O N D
Months of the year

Dublin
°C
Average temperature for year: 10°C
J F M A M J J A S O N D
Months of the year

Edinburgh
°C
Average temperature for year: 9°C
J F M A M J J A S O N D
Months of the year

London
°C
Average temperature for year: 11°C
J F M A M J J A S O N D
Months of the year

Plymouth
°C
Average temperature for year: 11°C
J F M A M J J A S O N D
Months of the year

Winter temperature

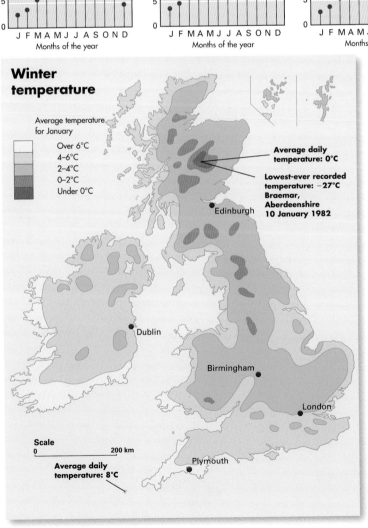

Average temperature for January

- Over 6°C
- 4–6°C
- 2–4°C
- 0–2°C
- Under 0°C

Average daily temperature: 0°C

Lowest-ever recorded temperature: −27°C Braemar, Aberdeenshire 10 January 1982

Edinburgh

Dublin

Birmingham

London

Scale
0   200 km

Average daily temperature: 8°C

Plymouth

Summer temperature

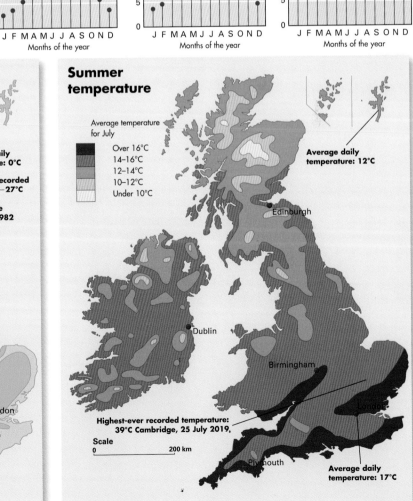

Average temperature for July

- Over 16°C
- 14–16°C
- 12–14°C
- 10–12°C
- Under 10°C

Average daily temperature: 12°C

Edinburgh

Dublin

Birmingham

London

Highest-ever recorded temperature: 39°C Cambridge, 25 July 2019.

Scale
0   200 km

Plymouth

Average daily temperature: 17°C

Water

Rainfall areas in the UK and Ireland

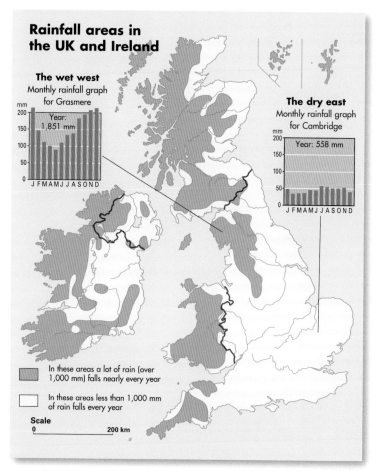

The wet west
Monthly rainfall graph for Grasmere

Year: 1,851 mm

mm
200
150
100
50
0
J F M A M J J A S O N D

The dry east
Monthly rainfall graph for Cambridge

Year: 558 mm

mm
200
150
100
50
0
J F M A M J J A S O N D

In these areas a lot of rain (over 1,000 mm) falls nearly every year

In these areas less than 1,000 mm of rain falls every year

Scale
0   200 km

Reservoirs and boreholes

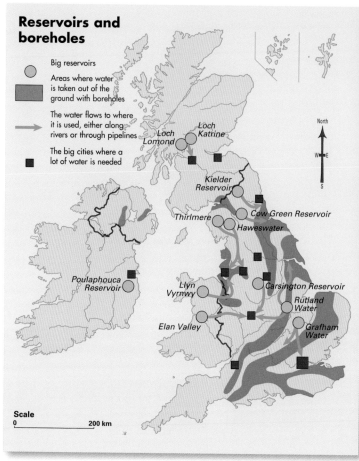

Big reservoirs

Areas where water is taken out of the ground with boreholes

The water flows to where it is used, either along rivers or through pipelines

The big cities where a lot of water is needed

North
W E
S

Loch Lomond
Loch Katrine
Kielder Reservoir
Thirlmere
Cow Green Reservoir
Haweswater
Poulaphouca Reservoir
Llyn Vyrnwy
Carsington Reservoir
Rutland Water
Elan Valley
Grafham Water

Scale
0   200 km

Sources of river pollution

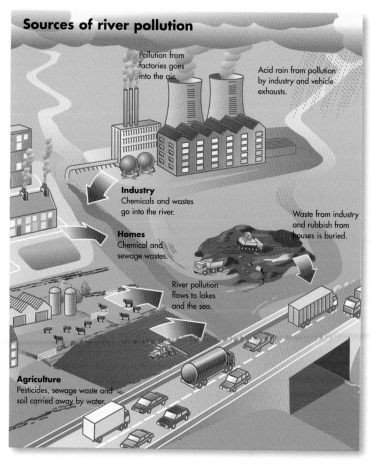

Pollution from factories goes into the air.

Acid rain from pollution by industry and vehicle exhausts.

Industry
Chemicals and wastes go into the river.

Homes
Chemical and sewage wastes.

Waste from industry and rubbish from houses is buried.

River pollution flows to lakes and the sea.

Agriculture
Pesticides, sewage waste and soil carried away by water.

Pollution

Percentage of rivers of very good quality

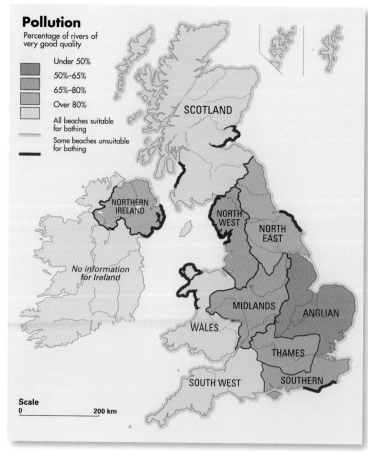

Under 50%
50%–65%
65%–80%
Over 80%

All beaches suitable for bathing
Some beaches unsuitable for bathing

SCOTLAND
NORTHERN IRELAND
NORTH WEST
NORTH EAST
No information for Ireland
MIDLANDS
ANGLIAN
WALES
THAMES
SOUTH WEST
SOUTHERN

Scale
0   200 km

Up to 17,400 million litres of water are used each day in the UK. Over half the water is used by people in their homes. About a third is used to make electricity. The rest is used in farms, fish farms and factories. In the UK each person uses about 150 litres of water per day. On the right are some of the ways that water is used in the home.

To make one car can use up to 40,000 litres of water. To brew one pint of beer needs 8 pints of water.

How we use water in the home

Flushing the toilet	30%
Showering and bathing	25%
Clothes washing	21%
Washing up	8%
Outdoors	7%
Drinking	4%

The water cycle

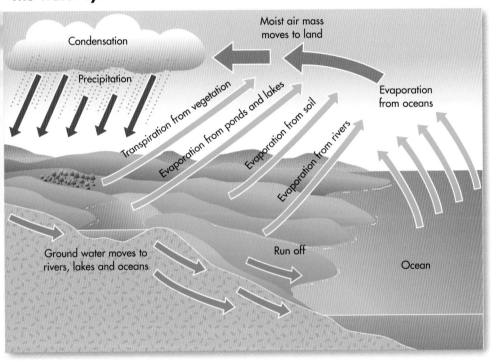

Flooding

Around 5 million people, in 2 million properties, live in flood risk areas in England and Wales. Periods of extreme rainfall can lead to widespread flooding.

The Environment Agency has an important role in warning people about the risk of flooding, and in reducing the likelihood of flooding from rivers and the sea.

Domestic water and sewage (the man-made water cycle)

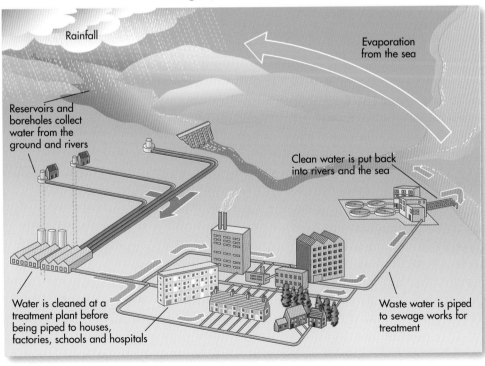

Flood risk in England and Wales

Areas at greatest risk from flooding

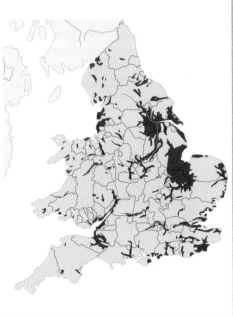

Farming and fishing

Types of farm in the UK and Ireland

Dairy farms
- Cows for milk, butter and cheese

Beef farms
- Cows and calves for beef and veal

Sheep farms
- Sheep and lambs for wool and meat

Grain and root farms
- Wheat, potatoes, sugar beet and oilseed rape

Mixed farms
- Livestock and grain or roots

Market gardening
- Vegetables, fruit and flowers

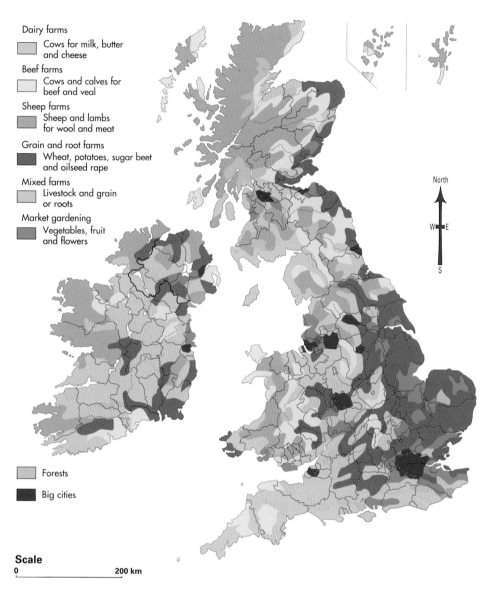

- Forests
- Big cities

Scale
0 — 200 km

Employment in agriculture

Percentage of the workforce employed in farming, forestry and fishing

- Over 10%
- 2–10%
- Under 10%

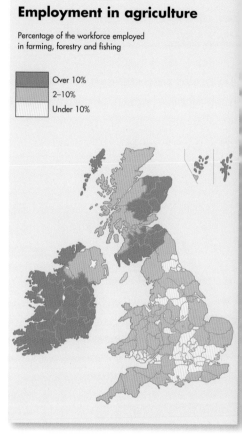

How much of our food is grown in the UK?

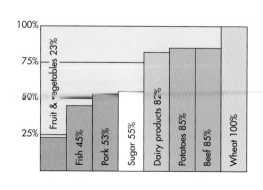

Fruit & Vegetables 23%
Fish 45%
Pork 53%
Sugar 55%
Dairy products 82%
Potatoes 85%
Beef 85%
Wheat 100%

(100%, 75%, 50%, 25%)

Where does the food eaten in the UK come from?

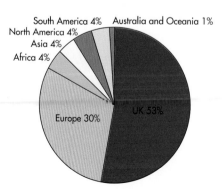

South America 4% Australia and Oceania 1%
North America 4%
Asia 4%
Africa 4%
Europe 30%
UK 53%

Fishing

- Large fishing ports (over 20,000 tonnes of fish caught each year)
- Other important fishing ports

Scrabster
Kinlochbervie
Ullapool
Fraserburgh
Lerwick
Peterhead
Mallaig
ATLANTIC OCEAN
NORTH SEA
Killybegs
Belfast
Kirkcudbright
North Shields
Portavogie
Scarborough
Kilkeel
Ardglass
Douglas
Bridlington
Grimsby
IRISH SEA
Dingle
Dunmore East
Milford Haven
Leigh-on-Sea
Castletown Bearhaven
CELTIC SEA
Shoreham
Plymouth
Brixham
Newlyn
ENGLISH CHANNEL

Conservation

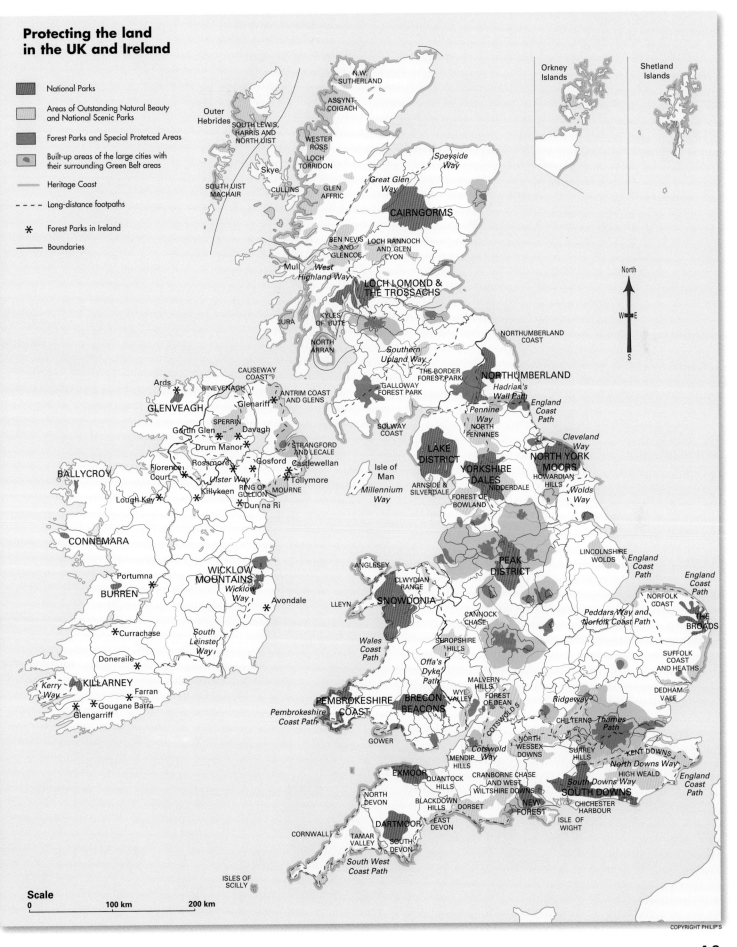

Protecting the land in the UK and Ireland

- National Parks
- Areas of Outstanding Natural Beauty and National Scenic Parks
- Forest Parks and Special Protected Areas
- Built-up areas of the large cities with their surrounding Green Belt areas
- Heritage Coast
- Long-distance footpaths
- * Forest Parks in Ireland
- Boundaries

Orkney Islands

Shetland Islands

Outer Hebrides

N.W. SUTHERLAND

ASSYNT-COIGACH

SOUTH LEWIS, HARRIS AND NORTH UIST

WESTER ROSS

LOCH TORRIDON

Skye

CULLINS

GLEN AFFRIC

SOUTH UIST MACHAIR

Speyside Way

Great Glen Way

CAIRNGORMS

BEN NEVIS AND GLENCOE

LOCH RANNOCH AND GLEN LYON

Mull

West Highland Way

LOCH LOMOND & THE TROSSACHS

JURA

KYLES OF BUTE

NORTH ARRAN

NORTHUMBERLAND COAST

Southern Upland Way

North

W—E

S

CAUSEWAY COAST

Ards

BINEVENAGH

ANTRIM COAST AND GLENS

GLENVEAGH

Glenariff

SPERRIN

Gortin Glen

Davagh

Drum Manor

Rossmore

Gosford

Florence Court

Castlewellan

STRANGFORD AND LECALE

THE BORDER FOREST PARK

GALLOWAY FOREST PARK

SOLWAY COAST

NORTHUMBERLAND

Hadrian's Wall Path

England Coast Path

Pennine Way

NORTH PENNINES

Cleveland Way

LAKE DISTRICT

NORTH YORK MOORS

HOWARDIAN HILLS

BALLYCROY

Lough Key

Ulster Way

Killykeen

RING OF GULLION

Tollymore

MOURNE

Dun na Ri

Isle of Man

Millennium Way

ARNSIDE & SILVERDALE

YORKSHIRE DALES

NIDDERDALE

FOREST OF BOWLAND

Wolds Way

CONNEMARA

Portumna

BURREN

WICKLOW MOUNTAINS

Wicklow Way

Avondale

South Leinster Way

Currachase

Doneraile

ANGLESEY

LLEYN

CLWYDIAN RANGE

SNOWDONIA

LINCOLNSHIRE WOLDS

England Coast Path

PEAK DISTRICT

NORFOLK COAST

England Coast Path

THE BROADS

CANNOCK CHASE

Peddars Way and Norfolk Coast Path

SHROPSHIRE HILLS

SUFFOLK COAST AND HEATHS

Wales Coast Path

Offa's Dyke Path

MALVERN HILLS

WYE VALLEY

FOREST OF DEAN

Ridgeway

DEDHAM VALE

Kerry Way

KILLARNEY

Farran

Gougane Barra

Glengarriff

PEMBROKESHIRE COAST

BRECON BEACONS

Pembrokeshire Coast Path

GOWER

MENDIP HILLS

Cotswold Way

COTSWOLDS

NORTH WESSEX DOWNS

CHILTERNS

Thames Path

SURREY HILLS

KENT DOWNS

North Downs Way

HIGH WEALD

South Downs Way

SOUTH DOWNS

England Coast Path

EXMOOR

QUANTOCK HILLS

CRANBORNE CHASE AND WEST WILTSHIRE DOWNS

NORTH DEVON

BLACKDOWN HILLS

DORSET

EAST DEVON

NEW FOREST

CHICHESTER HARBOUR

ISLE OF WIGHT

CORNWALL

TAMAR VALLEY

DARTMOOR

SOUTH DEVON

South West Coast Path

ISLES OF SCILLY

Scale

0   100 km   200 km

Work, industry and energy

Total workforce in the UK and Ireland

The number of people working

- Over 4 million
- 3–4 million
- 2–3 million
- Under 2 million

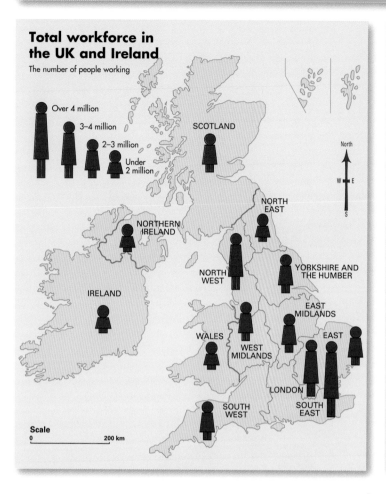

SCOTLAND
NORTH EAST
NORTHERN IRELAND
YORKSHIRE AND THE HUMBER
NORTH WEST
IRELAND
EAST MIDLANDS
WALES
WEST MIDLANDS
EAST
LONDON
SOUTH WEST
SOUTH EAST

North
W — E
S

Scale
0 — 200 km

Employment in service industries in the UK and Ireland

- Over 90%
- 85%–90%
- 82.5%–85%
- 80%–82.5%
- Under 80%

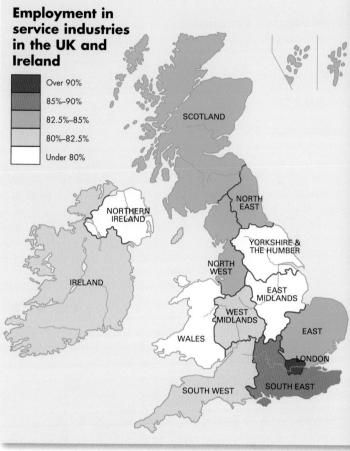

SCOTLAND
NORTH EAST
NORTHERN IRELAND
YORKSHIRE & THE HUMBER
NORTH WEST
IRELAND
EAST MIDLANDS
WEST MIDLANDS
EAST
LONDON
WALES
SOUTH WEST
SOUTH EAST

Manufacturing industries are industries which make things. Some examples of manufactured goods are cars, steel, textiles and clothes.

Service industries do not make things. They provide a service to people. Shops, hotels and banks are examples of service industries.

Unemployment

Percentage of the workforce unemployed in 2020

- Over 6%
- 5–6%
- 4–6%
- Under 4%

SCOTLAND
NORTHERN IRELAND
NORTH EAST
YORKSHIRE & THE HUMBER
NORTH WEST
IRELAND
EAST MIDLANDS
WEST MIDLANDS
EAST
WALES
LONDON
SOUTH WEST
SOUTH EAST

Employment in manufacturing

Percentage of the workforce employed in manufacturing in 2020

- Over 11%
- 10–11%
- 9–10%
- 7–9%
- 5–7%
- Under 5%

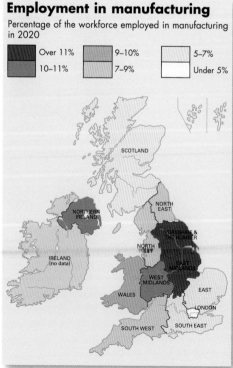

SCOTLAND
NORTH EAST
NORTHERN IRELAND
YORKSHIRE & THE HUMBER
NORTH WEST
IRELAND (no data)
EAST MIDLANDS
WEST MIDLANDS
EAST
WALES
LONDON
SOUTH WEST
SOUTH EAST

Income

The average amount each person earns each week in 2020

- Over £800
- £700–£800
- £625–£700
- £600–£625
- £550–£600

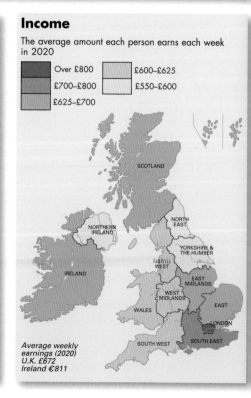

SCOTLAND
NORTHERN IRELAND
NORTH EAST
YORKSHIRE & THE HUMBER
NORTH WEST
IRELAND
EAST MIDLANDS
WEST MIDLANDS
EAST
WALES
LONDON
SOUTH WEST
SOUTH EAST

Average weekly earnings (2020)
U.K. £672
Ireland €811

Sources of energy used in the UK

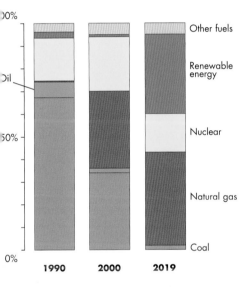

Bioenergy & heat 6% Coal 1%

Nuclear 18%

Oil 44%

Natural gas 31%

Total consumption in 2019
143 million tonnes of oil equivalent

Electricity generation in the UK (1990–2019)

)0%

Oil

50%

0%

1990   **2000**   **2019**

Other fuels

Renewable energy

Nuclear

Natural gas

Coal

This bar-chart shows the different types of fuel that are used to make electricity in the UK. The use of coal and oil in the generation of electricity has dropped between 1990 and 2019. However, the use of renewable energy has greatly increased.

Renewable energy in the UK

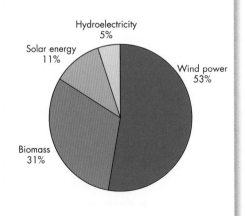

Hydroelectricity 5%

Solar energy 11%

Wind power 53%

Biomass 31%

Onshore and offshore windfarms are the largest source of renewable energy in the UK.

Energy sources in the UK and Ireland

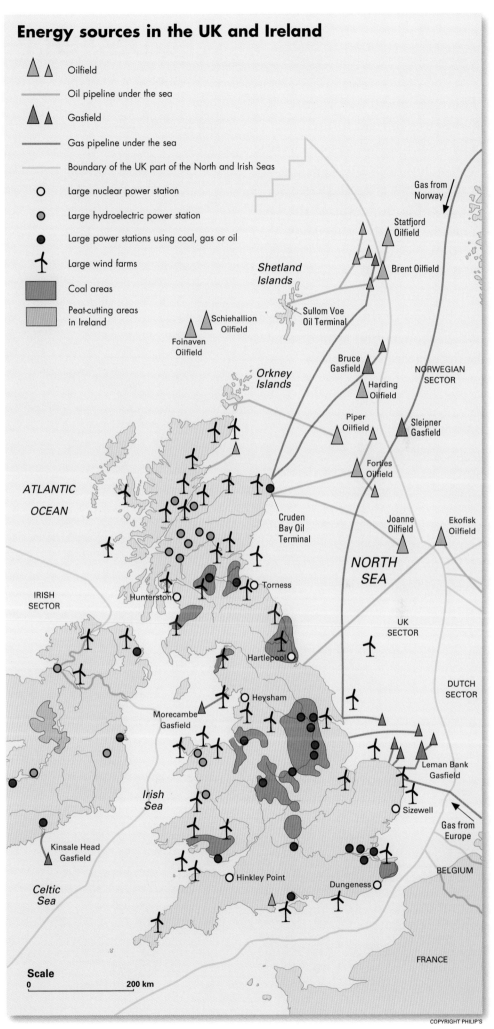

△ △ Oilfield

———— Oil pipeline under the sea

▲ ▲ Gasfield

———— Gas pipeline under the sea

———— Boundary of the UK part of the North and Irish Seas

○ Large nuclear power station

◐ Large hydroelectric power station

● Large power stations using coal, gas or oil

↟ Large wind farms

▮ Coal areas

▮ Peat-cutting areas in Ireland

Gas from Norway

Statfjord Oilfield

Brent Oilfield

Shetland Islands

Sullom Voe Oil Terminal

Schiehallion Oilfield

Foinaven Oilfield

NORWEGIAN SECTOR

Bruce Gasfield

Harding Oilfield

Orkney Islands

Piper Oilfield

Sleipner Gasfield

Forties Oilfield

ATLANTIC OCEAN

Cruden Bay Oil Terminal

Joanne Oilfield

Ekofisk Oilfield

NORTH SEA

IRISH SECTOR

Torness

Hunterston

UK SECTOR

Hartlepool

DUTCH SECTOR

Heysham

Morecambe Gasfield

Irish Sea

Leman Bank Gasfield

Sizewell

Gas from Europe

Kinsale Head Gasfield

BELGIUM

Hinkley Point

Dungeness

Celtic Sea

FRANCE

Scale
0   200 km

COPYRIGHT PHILIP'S

15

Transport

There are about 407 thousand kilometres of road in the UK. The total number of cars, buses, lorries and motorbikes is 38 million. That is more than half the number of people in the UK. The maps on this page show the motorways and some main roads in the UK and the number of cars in the different regions. At the bottom of the page there are tables showing the road distances between important towns.

Roads in the UK and Ireland

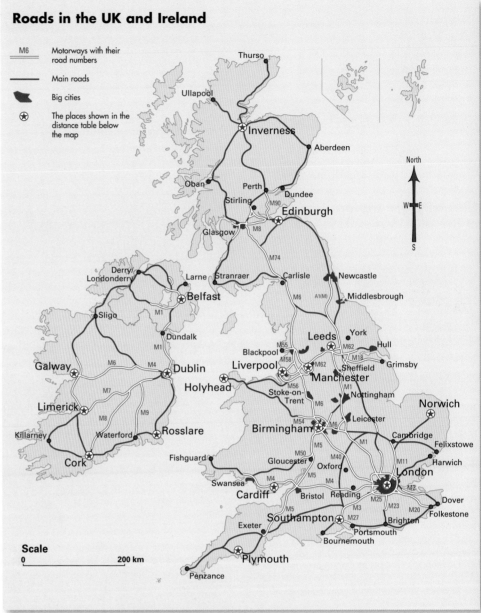

M6 (═══)	Motorways with their road numbers
──	Main roads
◆	Big cities
✹	The places shown in the distance table below the map

Scale
0 ———————— 200 km

Cars

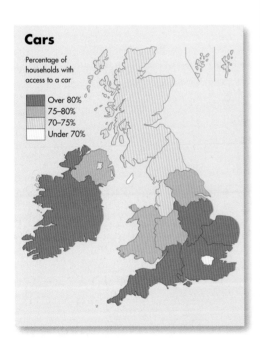

Percentage of households with access to a car

- Over 80%
- 75–80%
- 70–75%
- Under 70%

UK

UK	Birmingham	Cardiff	Edinburgh	Holyhead	Inverness	Leeds	Liverpool	London	Manchester	Norwich	Plymouth	Southampton
Birmingham		163	460	246	716	179	151	179	130	249	320	206
Cardiff	163		587	341	843	341	264	249	277	381	259	192
Edinburgh	460	587		489	256	320	338	608	336	586	790	669
Holyhead	246	341	489		745	262	151	420	198	481	528	455
Inverness	716	843	256	745		579	605	864	604	842	1049	925
Leeds	179	341	320	262	579		119	306	64	277	502	378
Liverpool	151	264	338	151	605	119		330	55	360	452	357
London	179	249	608	420	864	306	330		309	172	343	127
Manchester	130	277	336	198	604	64	55	309		306	457	325
Norwich	249	381	586	481	842	277	360	172	306		515	299
Plymouth	320	259	790	528	1049	502	452	343	457	515		246
Southampton	206	192	669	455	925	378	357	127	325	299	246	

Road distances

The distance tables are in kilometres, but distances on road signposts in the UK are in miles.
A mile is longer than a kilometre.
1 mile = 1.6 kilometres. 1 kilometre = 0.6 mile.

Ireland

Ireland	Belfast	Cork	Dublin	Galway	Limerick	Rosslare
Belfast		418	160	300	222	306
Cork	418		257	193	97	190
Dublin	160	257		210	193	137
Galway	300	193	210		97	249
Limerick	222	97	193	97		193
Rosslare	306	190	137	249	193	

Railways

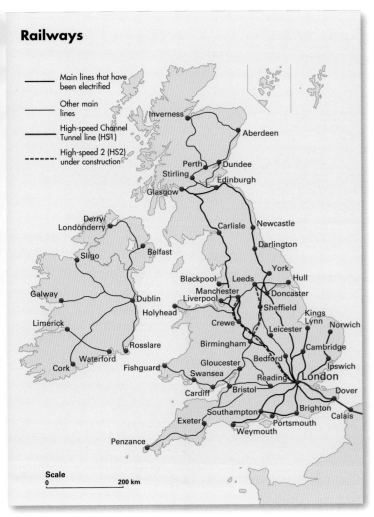

- ▬▬ Main lines that have been electrified
- ── Other main lines
- ▬▬ High-speed Channel Tunnel line (HS1)
- ┅┅ High-speed 2 (HS2) under construction

Scale
0 ─────── 200 km

Manchester – the daily flow of cars

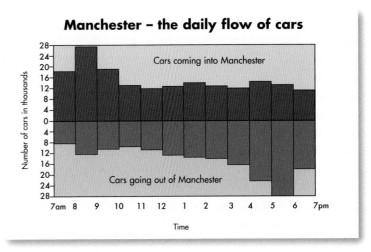

Cars coming into Manchester

Cars going out of Manchester

Number of cars in thousands

Time: 7am 8 9 10 11 12 1 2 3 4 5 6 7pm

High-speed rail

High-speed rail lines in Europe are shown in red on the map. Trains can travel at over 200 km/h on these lines.

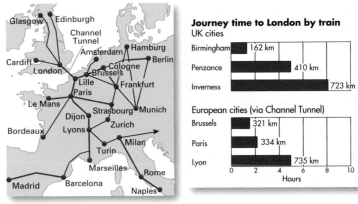

Journey time to London by train

UK cities
- Birmingham 162 km
- Penzance 410 km
- Inverness 723 km

European cities (via Channel Tunnel)
- Brussels 321 km
- Paris 334 km
- Lyon 735 km

Hours: 0 2 4 6 8 10

Ports and ferries

- 🚢 Major ports
- ⛴ Other ports
- ┄┄ Passenger ferries

Scale
0 ─────── 200 km

Airports

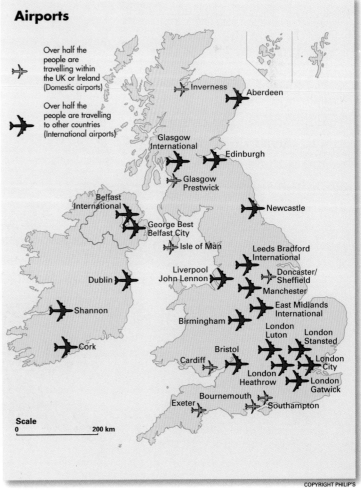

- ✈ Over half the people are travelling within the UK or Ireland (Domestic airports)
- ✈ Over half the people are travelling to other countries (International airports)

Scale
0 ─────── 200 km

Countries, regions and counties

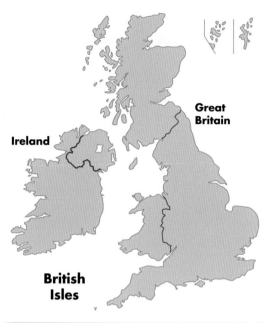

Great Britain

Ireland

British Isles

Country names

*The map on the left shows the **British Isles**, which is made up of the two large islands of **Great Britain** and **Ireland** and many smaller islands. The islands contain two countries, the **United Kingdom** and **Ireland**. The full name of the United Kingdom is The United Kingdom of Great Britain and Northern Ireland. It has four parts: **England**, **Wales**, **Scotland** and **Northern Ireland**. It is known for short as the United Kingdom, UK or Britain. The whole country is often wrongly called England. Ireland is sometimes shown as Eire (on its stamps), which is the name of Ireland in the Irish language.*

SCOTLAND
Edinburgh

NORTHERN IRELAND
Belfast

UNITED KINGDOM

ISLE OF MAN

Dublin

IRELAND

WALES   ENGLAND
Cardiff   London

• Capital cities

Countries and regions

The map shows the Standard Regions of the United Kingdom. The boundaries follow those of the counties shown on page 19. Large bodies like the Health Service and Water and Power providers divide the country up into their own regions. Ireland is divided into four historic provinces.

Scale
0 _____ 200 km

SCOTLAND

North
W—E
S

ULSTER
NORTHERN IRELAND
ULSTER
ULSTER
CONNAUGHT
IRELAND
LEINSTER
MUNSTER

ISLE OF MAN

NORTH EAST

YORKSHIRE AND HUMBERSIDE

NORTH WEST

EAST MIDLANDS

WEST MIDLANDS

EAST OF ENGLAND

WALES   **ENGLAND**

LONDON

SOUTH WEST   SOUTH EAST

CHANNEL ISLANDS

Counties and unitary authorities

England and Wales are divided into counties, unitary authorities and boroughs.

Scotland is divided into regions and unitary authorities, and Northern Ireland into districts.

Ireland is divided into counties.

Area data	
	Area in square kilometres
England	130,439
Wales	20,768
Scotland	77,167
Northern Ireland	13,483
United Kingdom	**241,857**
Isle of Man	**572**
Channel Islands	**195**
Ireland	**68,896**

SCOTLAND
1. ABERDEEN CITY
2. DUNDEE CITY
3. WEST DUNBARTONSHIRE
4. EAST DUNBARTONSHIRE
5. CITY OF GLASGOW
6. INVERCLYDE
7. RENFREWSHIRE
8. EAST RENFREWSHIRE
9. NORTH LANARKSHIRE
10. FALKIRK
11. CLACKMANNANSHIRE
12. WEST LOTHIAN
13. CITY OF EDINBURGH
14. MIDLOTHIAN

WALES
15. SWANSEA
16. NEATH PORT TALBOT
17. BRIDGEND
18. RHONDDA CYNON TAFF
19. MERTHYR TYDFIL
20. CAERPHILLY
21. BLAENAU GWENT
22. TORFAEN
23. CARDIFF
24. NEWPORT

ENGLAND
25. HARTLEPOOL
26. DARLINGTON
27. STOCKTON-ON-TEES
28. MIDDLESBROUGH
29. REDCAR AND CLEVELAND
30. BLACKPOOL
31. BLACKBURN WITH DARWEN
32. HALTON
33. WARRINGTON
34. KINGSTON UPON HULL
35. NORTH EAST LINCOLNSHIRE
36. CHESHIRE WEST AND CHESTER
37. CHESHIRE EAST
38. STOKE-ON-TRENT
39. TELFORD AND WREKIN
40. DERBY CITY
41. CITY OF NOTTINGHAM
42. LEICESTER CITY
43. RUTLAND
44. PETERBOROUGH
45. BEDFORD
46. MILTON KEYNES
47. CENTRAL BEDFORDSHIRE
48. LUTON
49. NORTH SOMERSET
50. CITY OF BRISTOL
51. BATH AND N. E. SOMERSET
52. SWINDON
53. READING
54. WOKINGHAM
55. WINDSOR AND MAIDENHEAD
56. SLOUGH
57. BRACKNELL FOREST
58. THURROCK
59. SOUTHEND-ON-SEA
60. MEDWAY
61. PLYMOUTH
62. TORBAY
63. BOURNEMOUTH,
    CHRISTCHURCH & POOLE
64. SOUTHAMPTON
65. PORTSMOUTH
66. BRIGHTON AND HOVE

Scale
0 — 100 km — 200 km

● Capital cities

19

People, cities and towns

Old people and young people

 In these counties, young people are a large group in the population (over 20%). On this map young people are those aged under 15 years old.

 In these counties, old people are a large group in the population (over 20%). On this map old people are those aged over 65 years old.

Look at the colours on the map above. Can you think of some reasons why some counties have more older people than others?

People in the UK and Ireland

Number of people per square kilometre in 2019

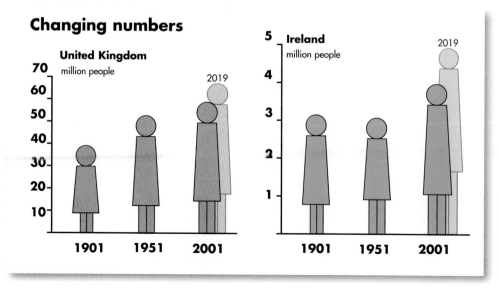

Over 1000
500–1000
200–500
100–200
50–100
25–50
Under 25

The average density for the U.K. is 275 people per km2.

The average density for Ireland is 70 people per km2.

Aberdeen

Edinburgh

Glasgow

Newcastle-upon-Tyne

Sunderland

Belfast

York

Bradford

Leeds

Kingston upon Hull

Manchester

Doncaster

Liverpool

Sheffield

Warrington

Stoke-on-Trent

Nottingham

Dublin

Wolverhampton

Derby

Leicester

Dudley

Coventry

Birmingham

Northampton

Milton Keynes

Luton

Swindon

Swansea

Cardiff

Bristol

London

Southampton

Brighton

Portsmouth

Plymouth

Populations of major cities

■ Over 5,000,000
● 1,000,000–5,000,000
■ 400,000–1,000,000
● 200,000–400,000
• 100,000–200,000

Country population data

	1901	1951	2019
		millions	
England	30.5	41.2	56.3
Wales	2.0	2.6	3.2
Scotland	4.5	5.1	5.5
Northern Ireland	1.2	1.4	1.9
United Kingdom	**38.2**	**50.3**	**66.8**
Ireland	**3.2**	**2.9**	**4.9**

Changing numbers

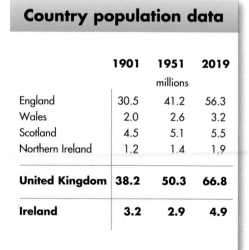

United Kingdom
million people

70
60
50
40
30
20
10

2019

1901 1951 2001

Ireland
million people

5
4
3
2
1

2019

1901 1951 2001

Cities and towns of the UK and Ireland

Map scale   This distance is 400 kilometres

0 ————————————————————— 400 km

Map information

Height of land

	metres
	Over 1,000
	500–1,000
	200–500
	0–200
	Below sea level
	Sea

Cities and towns

London ■	Over 9,000,000 people
Dublin ■	1,000,000 – 9,000,000 people
Leeds ●	500,000 – 1,000,000 people
Plymouth ●	200,000 – 500,000 people
Oxford ●	100,000 – 200,000 people
Guildford ●	50,000 – 100,000 people
Dover ·	Under 50,000 people

Shetland Islands

Lerwick

Orkney Islands

Kirkwall

ATLANTIC OCEAN

Thurso
Wick
Helmsdale
Stornoway
Lairg
Golspie
Ullapool
Invergordon
Dingwall
Banff
Fraserburgh
Peterhead
Nairn
Elgin
Huntly
Inverness
Inverurie
Aviemore
Aberdeen
S C O T L A N D
Mallaig
Ballater
Stonehaven
Portree
Tobermory
Fort William
Forfar
Montrose
Arbroath
Oban
Dundee
Perth
St. Andrews
Stirling
Glenrothes
Dunfermline
Kirkcaldy
Dumbarton
Dunbar
Greenock
Glasgow
Edinburgh
Paisley
Berwick-upon-Tweed
East Kilbride
Hamilton
Galashiels
Irvine
Kilmarnock
Jedburgh
Alnwick
Campbeltown
Ayr
Hawick

Outer Hebrides
Inner Hebrides

North

W—E
S

Girvan
Dumfries
Newcastle-upon-Tyne
Stranraer
South Shields
Buncrana
Coleraine
Gateshead
Sunderland
Letterkenny
Ballymena
Larne
Carlisle
Durham
Hartlepool
NORTHERN IRELAND
Antrim
Bangor
Workington
Darlington
Redcar
Donegal
Omagh
Portadown
Belfast
Whitehaven
Stockton
Middlesbrough
Bundoran
Enniskillen
Lurgan
Lisburn
Armagh
Newry
Scarborough
Ballina
Sligo
Barrow-in-Furness
Bridlington
Cavan
Douglas
Isle of Man
Lancaster
Harrogate
Castlebar
Dundalk
KINGDOM
York
Kingston upon Hull
Westport
Drogheda
Keighley
Leeds
Roscommon
Longford
Irish
Blackpool
Burnley
Bradford
Athlone
Mullingar
Preston
Halifax
Huddersfield
Scunthorpe
Galway
Tullamore
Blackburn
Barnsley
Grimsby
Ballinasloe
Birr
Dublin
Holyhead
Sea
Bolton
Doncaster
Manchester
Oldham
Rotherham
Lincoln
Ennis
Portlaoise
Dun Laoghaire
Liverpool
Stockport
Sheffield
Louth
I R E L A N D
Bray
Chester
Warrington
Skegness
Nenagh
Carlow
Bangor
Crewe
Chesterfield
Mansfield
Boston
Limerick
Thurles
Kilkenny
Arklow
Wrexham
Derby
Cromer
Tralee
Tipperary
Pwllheli
Stoke-on-Trent
Nottingham
King's Lynn
Clonmel
Carrick-on-Suir
Wexford
Shrewsbury
Stafford
Grantham
Great Yarmouth
Dingle
Mallow
Waterford
Rosslare Harbour
Telford
E N G L A N D
Norwich
Killarney
Dungarvan
Fishguard
Aberystwyth
Welshpool
Nuneaton
Leicester
Peterborough
Thetford
Lowestoft
Bantry
Bandon
Youghal
Cobh
Wolverhampton
Corby
Cork
Carmarthen
Birmingham
Rugby
Cambridge
Ely
Bury St. Edmunds
Ipswich
Haverfordwest
Merthyr Tydfil
Coventry
Northampton
Felixstowe
Milford Haven
Neath
Llanelli
Rhondda
Cwmbran
Worcester
Bedford
Harwich
Pembroke
Swansea
Port Talbot
Newport
Hereford
Milton Keynes
Stevenage
Colchester
Chelmsford
WALES
Brecon
Cheltenham
Oxford
Luton
Harlow
Gloucester
High Wycombe
Watford
Basildon
Southend
Cardiff
Swindon
Slough
Barry
Bristol
Newbury
Reading
London
Chatham
Bath
Margate
Weston-super-Mare
Basingstoke
Guildford
Reigate
Canterbury
Maidstone
Dover
Barnstaple
Salisbury
Winchester
Crawley
Ashford
Folkestone
Bude
Taunton
Yeovil
Southampton
Havant
Hastings
Eastbourne
Boulogne-sur-Mer
Newquay
Exeter
Bournemouth
Newport
Portsmouth
Brighton
Truro
Torquay
Poole
Weymouth
Worthing
St. Austell
Plymouth
Falmouth
Penzance
Calais
FRANCE

N o r t h   S e a

Celtic Sea

West from Greenwich   East from Greenwich

COPYRIGHT PHILIP'S

21

Tourism

Tourism in the UK and Ireland

- ● Main holiday destinations
- ● Other major tourist attractions

Scale
0   200 km

UK tourist attractions
(number of visitors in millions, 2019)

1. British Museum, London	6.2
2. Tate Modern, London	6.1
3. National Gallery, London	6.0
4. Natural History Museum, London	5.4
5. Southbank Centre, London	4.4
6. Victoria and Albert Museum, London	4.0
7. Science Museum, London	3.3
8. Tower of London	3.0
9. Royal Museums, Greenwich	2.9
10. Somerset House, London	2.8
11. Royal Botanic Gardens, Kew	2.3
12. National Museum of Scotland, Edinburgh	2.2
13. Edinburgh Castle	2.2
14. Chester Zoo	2.1
15. Kelvingrove Art Gallery & Museum, Glasgow	1.8
16. Tate Britain, London	1.8
17. Royal Albert Hall, London	1.7
18. St Paul's Cathedral, London	1.7
19. National Portrait Gallery, London	1.6
20. Stonehenge, Wiltshire	1.6

Ireland tourist attractions
(number of visitors in millions, 2019)

1. Guinness Storehouse, Dublin	1.7
2. Cliffs of Moher, Clare	1.6
3. Dublin Zoo	1.3
4. Book of Kells, Dublin	1.1
5. Castletown House Parklands, Kildare	1.0
6. Kilkenny Castle Parklands	0.9
7. National Gallery, Dublin	0.8
8. Glendalough Site, Wicklow	0.7
9. Tayto Park, Meath	0.7
10. National Botanic Gardens, Dublin	0.7

Tourist traffic

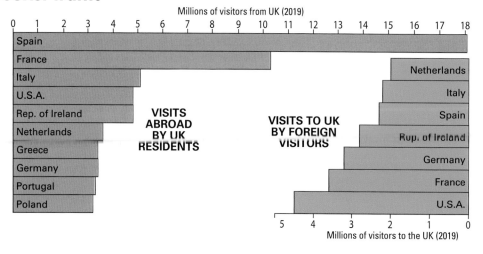

World tourist attractions
(number of foreign visitors in millions, 2019)

1. France	89.4
2. Spain	82.8
3. USA	79.6
4. China	62.9
5. Italy	62.1
6. Turkey	45.8
7. Mexico	41.4
8. Germany	38.9
9. Thailand	38.3
10. UK	36.3

International organizations

United Nations

The UN is the largest international organization in the world. The headquarters are in New York and 193 countries are members. It was formed in 1945 to help solve world problems and to help keep world peace. The UN sends peacekeeping forces to areas where there are problems.

★ Current UN peacekeeping forces

▨ UN member countries

Population
(million people)

Austria	9
Belgium	12
Bulgaria	7
Croatia	4
Cyprus	1
Czechia	11
Denmark	6
Estonia	1
Finland	6
France	68
Germany	80
Greece	11
Hungary	10
Ireland	5
Italy	62
Latvia	2
Lithuania	3
Luxembourg	0.6
Malta	0.5
Netherlands	17
Poland	38
Portugal	10
Romania	21
Slovakia	5
Slovenia	2
Spain	47
Sweden	10

European Union

▨ EU member countries

The EU was first formed in 1951. Six countries were members. Now there are 27 countries in the EU. These countries meet to discuss agriculture, industry and trade as well as social and political issues. The headquarters are in Brussels. Cyprus, Czechia, Estonia, Hungary, Latvia, Lithuania, Malta, Poland, Slovakia and Slovenia joined the EU in 2004. Bulgaria and Romania joined in 2007, Croatia in 2013. The UK left in 2020.

The Commonwealth

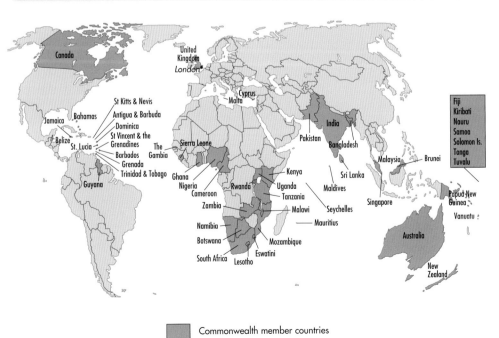

▨ Commonwealth member countries

The Commonwealth is a group of 54 independent countries which used to belong to the British Empire. It is organized by a group of people called the Secretariat which is based in London. Queen Elizabeth II is the head of the Commonwealth. About every two years the heads of the different governments meet to discuss world problems. These meetings are held in different countries in the Commonwealth.

England and Wales

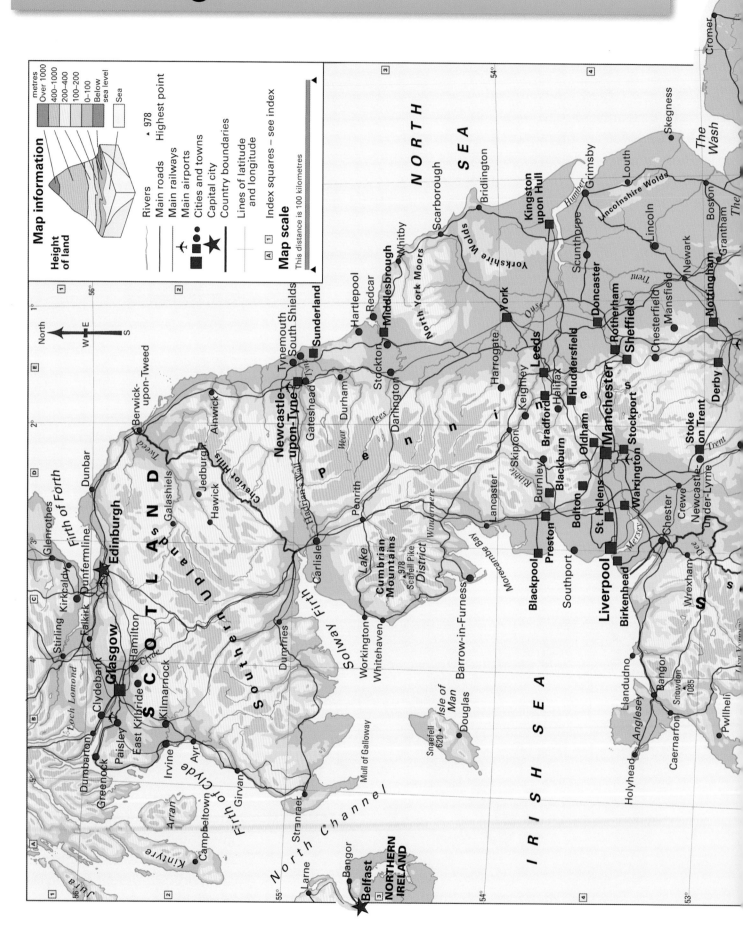

North
N W—E S
S

NORTH SEA

IRISH SEA

North Channel

NORTHERN IRELAND

SCOTLAND

Southern Uplands

Cheviot Hills

Pennines

Cumbrian Mountains
Lake District

Yorkshire Wolds
North York Moors
Lincolnshire Wolds

Isle of Man

Anglesey

Cromer
Skegness
The Wash
Louth
Boston
Grantham
Lincoln
Newark
Grimsby
Scunthorpe
Kingston upon Hull
Bridlington
Scarborough
Whitby
Doncaster
Nottingham
Mansfield
Chesterfield
Rotherham
Sheffield
Derby
Stoke on Trent
Newcastle-under-Lyme
Crewe
Chester
Wrexham
Llandudno
Bangor
Caernarfon
Holyhead
Pwllheli
Snowdon ▲ 1085
York
Harrogate
Leeds
Bradford
Keighley
Skipton
Halifax
Huddersfield
Oldham
Manchester
Stockport
Warrington
Bolton
St. Helens
Liverpool
Birkenhead
Southport
Blackburn
Burnley
Preston
Blackpool
Lancaster
Morecambe Bay
Barrow-in-Furness
Whitehaven
Workington
Penrith
Carlisle
Scafell Pike ▲ 978
Windermere
Ribble
Mersey
Dee
Ouse
Humber
Trent
Trent

Berwick-upon-Tweed
Alnwick
Newcastle upon-Tyne
Tynemouth
South Shields
Sunderland
Gateshead
Hadrian's Wall
Durham
Hartlepool
Redcar
Middlesbrough
Stockton
Darlington
Tyne
Wear
Tees

Edinburgh
Firth of Forth
Dunfermline
Kirkcaldy
Glenrothes
Stirling
Falkirk
Dunbar
Galashiels
Jedburgh
Hawick
Tweed
Dumfries
Solway Firth

Glasgow
Hamilton
Clydebank
Paisley
Greenock
Dumbarton
East Kilbride
Kilmarnock
Irvine
Ayr
Girvan
Stranraer
Campbeltown
Loch Lomond
Clyde
Firth of Clyde
Mull of Galloway
Arran
Kintyre
Jura

Larne
Bangor
Belfast

Douglas
Snaefell ▲ 620

54°
53°
54°
55°

1°
1°
2°
3°
4°
56°

[E] [D] [C] [B] [A]
[1] [2]
[3] [4]

24

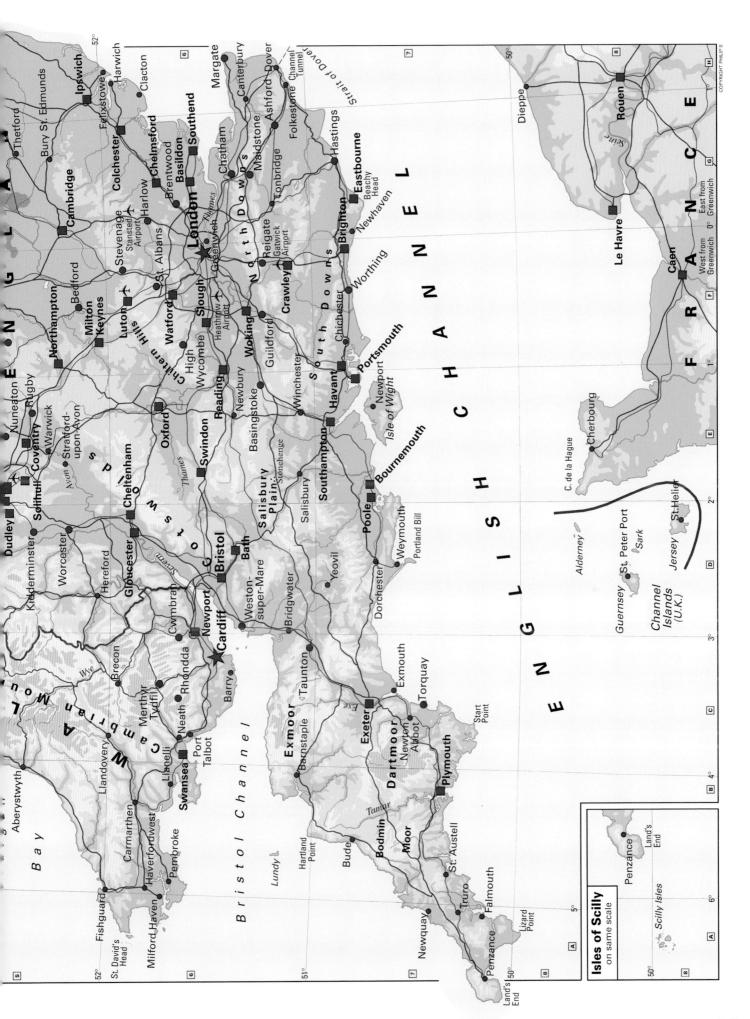

Isles of Scilly
on same scale

25

Scotland and Ireland

Orkney Islands
on same scale

Westray
Sanday
Rousay
Stronsay
Mainland
Kirkwall
Hoy
South
Ronaldsay
Pentland Firth
John o' Groats

Cape Wrath
Thurso
John o' Groats
Wick
Helmsdale
Lairg
Ullapool
Golspie
North West Highlands
Invergordon
Moray Firth
Elgin
Banff
Fraserburgh
Dingwall
Keith
Peterhead
Nairn
Inverness
Huntly
Spey
Inverurie
Dyce
Glen Mor
Aviemore
Westhill
Aberdeen
Cairn Gorm 1245
Don
Loch Ness
Ballater
Dee
Stonehaven
Grampian Mountains
Pitlochry
Montrose
Ben Nevis 1345
Forfar
Fort William
Arbroath
Glen Coe
Tay
Dundee
NORTH
Crianlarich
Perth
St. Andrews
SEA
Oban
Callander
Loch Awe
Glenrothes
Firth of Forth
Loch Lomond
Stirling
Kirkcaldy
Dumbarton
Cumbernauld
Dunfermline
Dunbar
Clydebank
Falkirk
Glasgow
Edinburgh
Greenock
Paisley
Hamilton
Berwick-upon-Tweed
Bute
East Kilbride
Tweed
Galashiels
Irvine
Kilmarnock
Troon
Clyde
Southern Uplands
Jedburgh
Ayr
Hawick
Alnwick
Cheviot Hills
Girvan
Lockerbie
Dumfries
Hadrian's Wall
Hexham
Carlisle
ENGLAND
Wear
West from Greenwich

Lewis
Stornoway
Outer Hebrides
Harris
North Uist
Benbecula
South Uist
Inner Hebrides
Portree
Skye
Kyle of Lochalsh
Mallaig
Barra
Rùm
Eigg
Coll
Tobermory
Tiree
Staffa
Mull
Iona
ATLANTIC
Colonsay
OCEAN
Jura
Islay
Kintyre
Arran
Campbeltown
Mull of Kintyre
Firth of Clyde
North Channel
NORTHERN IRELAND
Larne
Stranraer
Carrickfergus
Solway Firth

Shetland Islands
on same scale

Unst
Yell
Fetlar
Sullom Voe
Mainland
Foula
Lerwick

Map scale
This distance is 100 kilometres

COPYRIGHT PHILIP'S

26

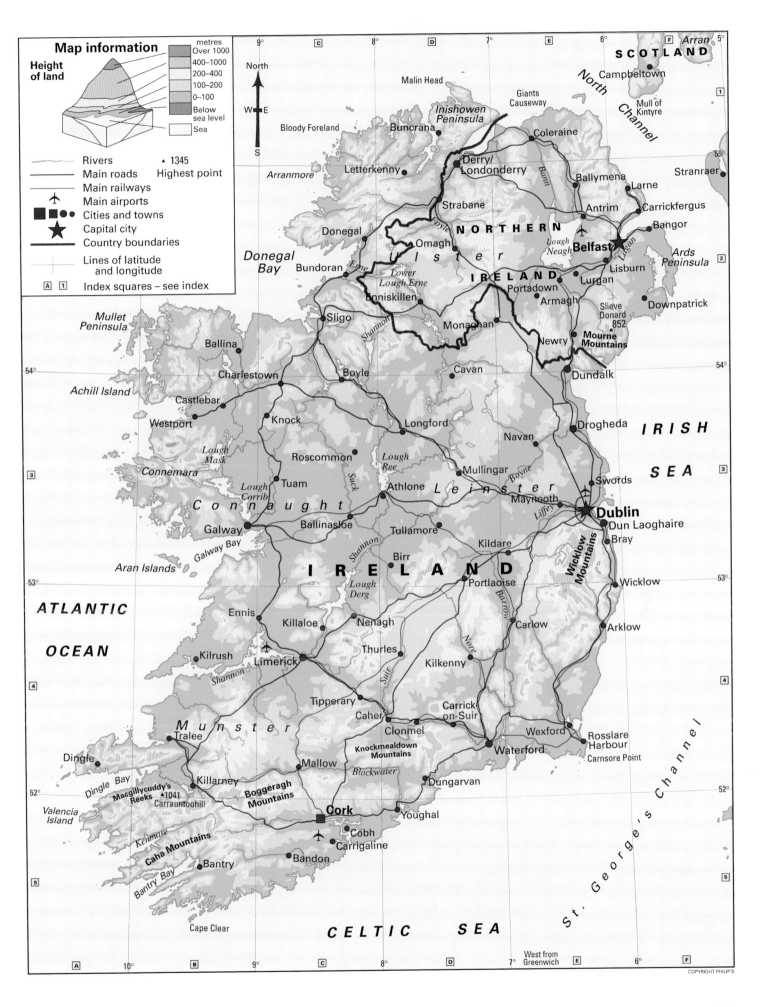

Map information

Height of land

metres
Over 1000
400–1000
200–400
100–200
0–100
Below sea level
Sea

North
W—E
S

Rivers
Main roads
Main railways
✈ Main airports
■ ■ ● ● Cities and towns
★ Capital city
Country boundaries
Lines of latitude and longitude
Ⓐ ① Index squares – see index

▲ 1345 Highest point

SCOTLAND
Campbeltown
Mull of Kintyre
Arran

North Channel

Malin Head
Giants Causeway
Coleraine
Stranraer
Bloody Foreland
Buncrana
Inishowen Peninsula
Derry/Londonderry
Ballymena
Larne
Carrickfergus
Letterkenny
Strabane
Antrim
Bangor
Arranmore
Donegal
Omagh
NORTHERN
Lough Neagh
Belfast
Lisburn
Ards Peninsula
Donegal Bay
Bundoran
Enniskillen
Lower Lough Erne
IRELAND
Portadown
Lurgan
Armagh
Downpatrick
Mullet Peninsula
Sligo
Monaghan
Slieve Donard 852
Newry
▲ Mourne Mountains
Dundalk
Ballina
Boyle
Cavan
Achill Island
Charlestown
Castlebar
Knock
Longford
Navan
Drogheda
IRISH SEA
Westport
Lough Mask
Roscommon
Lough Ree
Mullingar
Connemara
Lough Corrib
Tuam
Suck
Athlone
Boyne
Swords
CONNAUGHT
Ballinasloe
Tullamore
Maynooth
Dublin
Galway
Birr
Liffey
Dun Laoghaire
Galway Bay
Shannon
Kildare
Bray
Aran Islands
IRELAND
Portlaoise
Wicklow Mountains
Wicklow
Lough Derg
Barrow
Nore
Ennis
Killaloe
Nenagh
Carlow
Arklow
ATLANTIC
Kilrush
Thurles
OCEAN
Limerick
Kilkenny
Shannon
Tipperary
Suir
Munster
Caher
Carrick-on-Suir
Wexford
Tralee
Clonmel
Rosslare Harbour
Dingle
Knockmealdown Mountains
Waterford
Carnsore Point
Dingle Bay
Mallow
Blackwater
Dungarvan
Valencia Island
Killarney
Boggeragh Mountains
Macgillycuddy's Reeks ▲1041
Carrauntoohill
Youghal
Kenmare
Cork
Cobh
Caha Mountains
Carrigaline
Bantry
Bandon
Bantry Bay
Cape Clear

CELTIC SEA

St. George's Channel

West from Greenwich
COPYRIGHT PHILIP'S

27

The Earth as a planet

Relative sizes of the planets

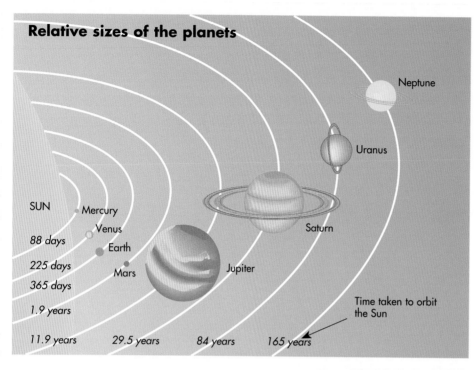

Neptune

Uranus

Saturn

SUN

Mercury

Venus

88 days

Earth

225 days

Mars

Jupiter

365 days

1.9 years

Time taken to orbit
the Sun

11.9 years   29.5 years   84 years   165 years

The Solar System

The Earth is one of the eight planets that orbit the Sun. These two diagrams show how big the planets are, how far they are away from the Sun and how long they take to orbit the Sun. The diagram on the left shows how the planets closest to the Sun have the shortest orbits. The Earth takes 365 days (a year) to go round the Sun. The Earth is the fifth largest planet. It is much smaller than Jupiter and Saturn which are the largest planets.

Distances of the planets from the Sun in millions of kilometres

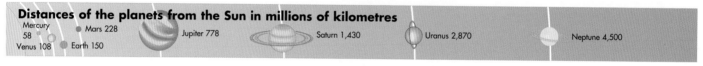

Mercury
58

Mars 228

Jupiter 778

Saturn 1,430

Uranus 2,870

Neptune 4,500

Venus 108   Earth 150

Planet Earth

The Earth spins as if it is on a rod – its axis. The axis would come out of the Earth at two points. The northern point is called the North Pole and the southern point is called the South Pole. The distance between the Poles through the centre of the Earth is 12,700 km.

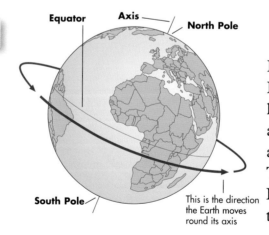

Equator   Axis   North Pole

South Pole

This is the direction
the Earth moves
round its axis

It takes a day (24 hours) for the Earth to rotate on its axis. It is light (day) when it faces the Sun and dark (night) when it faces away. See the diagram below. The Equator is a line round the Earth which is halfway between the Poles. It is 40,000 km long.

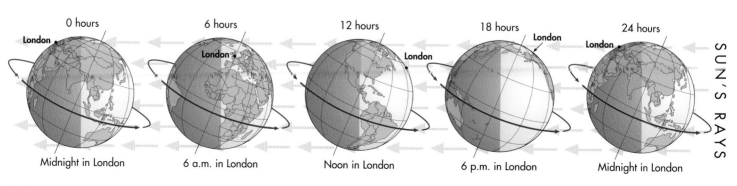

0 hours
London

6 hours
London

12 hours
London

18 hours
London

24 hours
London

Midnight in London   6 a.m. in London   Noon in London   6 p.m. in London   Midnight in London

SUN'S RAYS

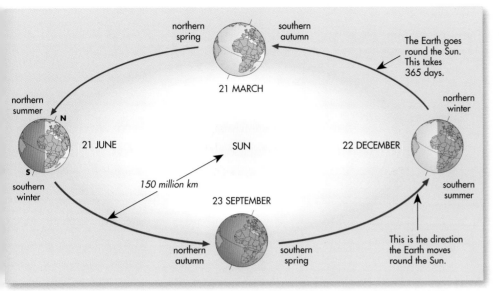

The Earth is always tilted at 23½°. It moves around the Sun. This movement gives us the seasons of the year. In June the northern hemisphere tilts towards the Sun so it is summer. Six months later, in December, the Earth has rotated halfway round the Sun. It is then summer in the southern hemisphere.

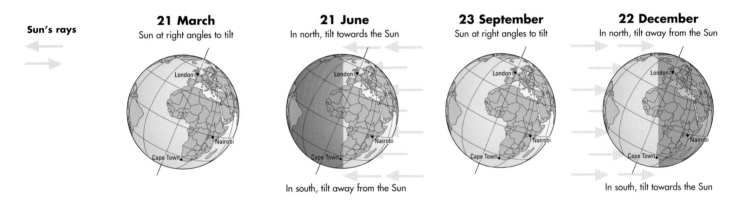

Season	Northern spring Southern autumn			Northern summer Southern winter			Northern autumn Southern spring			Northern winter Southern summer		
City	London	Nairobi	Cape Town	London	Nairobi	Cape Town	London	Nairobi	Cape Town	London	Nairobi	Cape Town
Latitude	51°N	1°S	34°S	51°N	1°S	34°S	51°N	1°S	34°S	51°N	1°S	34°S
Day length	12 hrs	12 hrs	12 hrs	16 hrs	12 hrs	10 hrs	12 hrs	12 hrs	12 hrs	8 hrs	12 hrs	14 hrs
Night length	12 hrs	12 hrs	12 hrs	8 hrs	12 hrs	14 hrs	12 hrs	12 hrs	12 hrs	16 hrs	12 hrs	10 hrs
Temperature	7°C	21°C	21°C	16°C	18°C	13°C	15°C	19°C	14°C	5°C	19°C	20°C

The Moon

The Moon is about a quarter the size of the Earth. It orbits the Earth in just over 27 days (almost a month). The Moon is round but we on Earth see only the parts lit by the Sun. This makes it look as if the Moon is a different shape at different times of the month. These are known as the phases of the Moon and they are shown in this diagram.

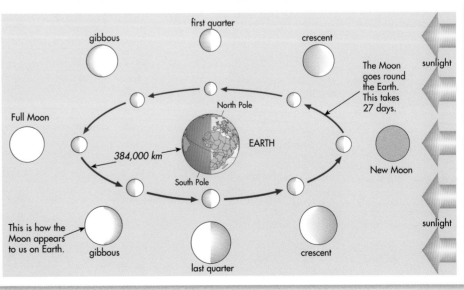

Mountains, seas and rivers

Over 70% of the surface of the Earth is covered with water and ice. Most of the mountain ranges have been formed by movements in the Earth's crust. They are coloured brown on the map. Rivers shape the landscape as they flow to the sea.

Largest oceans

(thousand square kilometres)

1. Pacific Ocean . . 155,557
2. Atlantic Ocean . . 76,762
3. Indian Ocean . . . 68,556
4. Southern Ocean . . 20,237
5. Arctic Ocean . . . 14,351

Largest seas

(thousand square kilometres)

1. Mediterranean Sea 2,966
2. South China Sea 2,318
3. Bering Sea 2,274
4. Caribbean Sea . . . 1,942
5. Gulf of Mexico . . . 1,813
6. Sea of Okhotsk . . . 1,528

Highest mountains

(metres)

Asia: Mt Everest 8,849
South America:
   Aconcagua 6,962
North America:
   Denali 6,190
Africa: Kilimanjaro . . 5,895
Europe: Elbrus 5,642

The course of a river

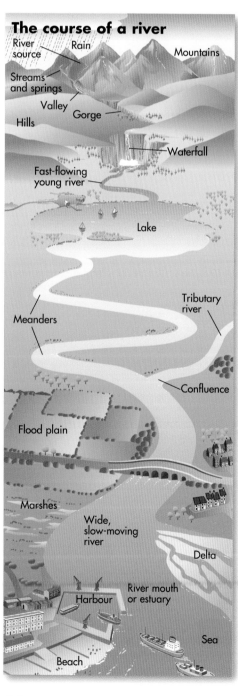

Largest lakes	Longest rivers	Largest islands	Deepest trenches
(thousand square kilometres)	(kilometres)	(thousand square kilometres)	(metres)
1. Caspian Sea 371	1. Nile 6,695	1. Greenland 2,176	1. Mariana Trench 11,022
2. Lake Superior. 82	2. Amazon 6,450	2. New Guinea. 821	2. Tonga Trench 10,822
3. Lake Victoria 68	3. Yangtse 6,380	3. Borneo 744	3. Japan Trench 10,554
4. Lake Huron 60	4. Mississippi 5,971	4. Madagascar 587	4. Kuril Trench 10,542
5. Lake Michigan 58	5. Yenisey. 5,550	5. Baffin Island. 508	5. Mindanao Trench . .10,497
6. Lake Tanganyika 33	6. Hwang-Ho 5,464	6. Sumatra 474	6. Kermadec Trench . .10,047
7. Great Bear Lake. 32	7. Ob 5,410	7. Honshu 231	7. Bougainville Trench . .9,140
8. Lake Baikal 31	8. Congo 4,670	8. Great Britain 230	8. Milwaukee Deep 8,605
9. Lake Malawi. 30	9. Mekong 4,500	9. Victoria Island 212	9. South Sandwich Trench 8,325
10. Great Salt Lake 29	10. Amur 4,442	10. Ellesmere Island. 197	10. Aleutian Trench 7,822

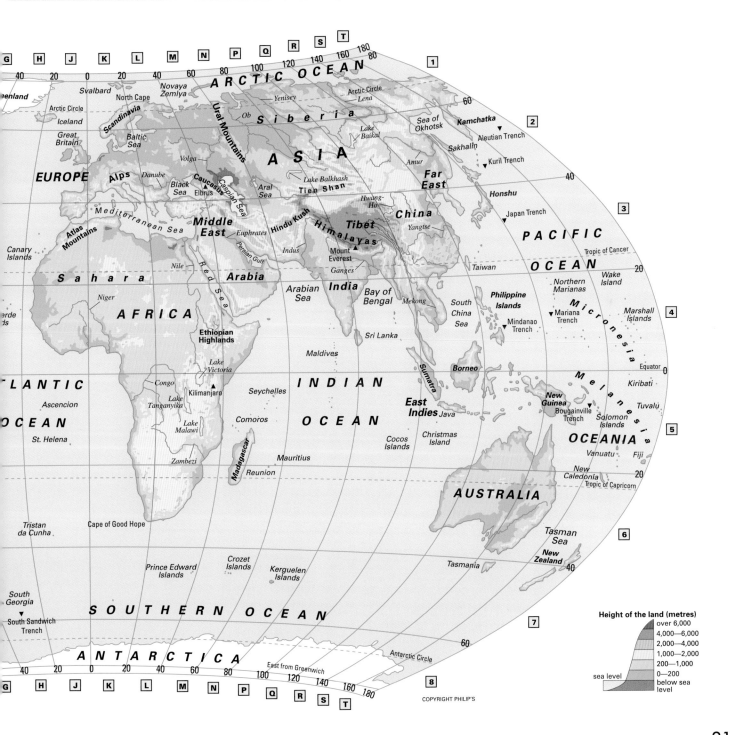

COPYRIGHT PHILIP'S

Height of the land (metres)

over 6,000
4,000—6,000
2,000—4,000
1,000—2,000
200—1,000
0—200
sea level
below sea level

31

Climate

Key to the climate map

■ Tropical climate (hot and wet)	□ Dry climate (desert and steppe)	▨ Mild climate (warm and wet)	▨ Continental climate (cold and wet)	▨ Polar climate (very cold and dry)	▨ Mountainous areas (where altitude affects climate type)

Heavy rainfall and high temperatures all the year with little difference between the hot and cold months.

Many months, often years, without rain. High temperatures in the summer but cooler in winter.

Rain every month. Warm summers and cool winters.

Mild summers and very cold winters.

Very cold at all times, especially in the winter months. Very little rainfall.

Lower temperatures because the land is high. Heavy rain and snow.

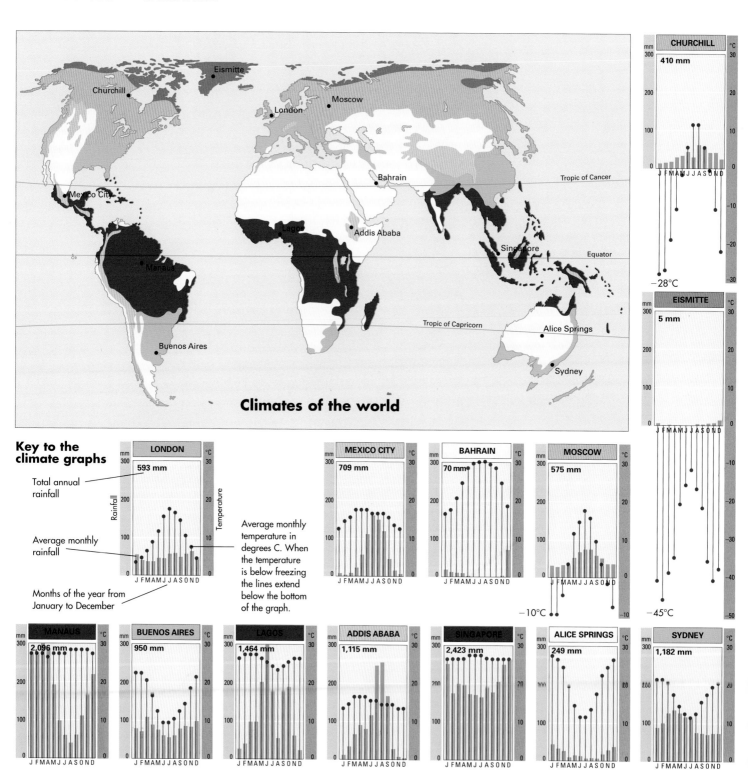

Climates of the world

Key to the climate graphs

Total annual rainfall

Average monthly rainfall

Months of the year from January to December

Average monthly temperature in degrees C. When the temperature is below freezing the lines extend below the bottom of the graph.

Annual rainfall

Human, plant and animal life cannot live without water. The map on the right shows how much rain falls in different parts of the world. You can see that there is a lot of rain in some places near the Equator. In other places, like the desert areas of the world, there is very little rain. Few plants or animals can survive there. There is also very little rain in the cold lands of the north.

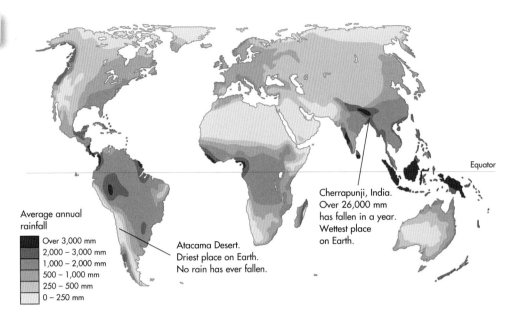

Equator

Average annual rainfall
- Over 3,000 mm
- 2,000 – 3,000 mm
- 1,000 – 2,000 mm
- 500 – 1,000 mm
- 250 – 500 mm
- 0 – 250 mm

Cherrapunji, India. Over 26,000 mm has fallen in a year. Wettest place on Earth.

Atacama Desert. Driest place on Earth. No rain has ever fallen.

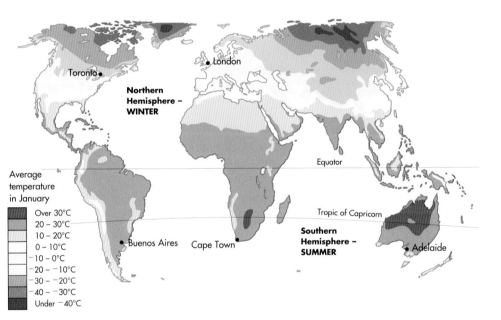

Toronto
London
Northern Hemisphere – WINTER
Equator

Average temperature in January
- Over 30°C
- 20 – 30°C
- 10 – 20°C
- 0 – 10°C
- −10 – 0°C
- −20 – −10°C
- −30 – −20°C
- −40 – −30°C
- Under −40°C

Buenos Aires
Cape Town
Tropic of Capricorn
Southern Hemisphere – SUMMER
Adelaide

January temperature

In December, it is winter in the northern hemisphere. It is hot in the southern continents and cold in the northern continents. The North Pole is tilted away from the sun. It is overhead in the regions around the Tropic of Capricorn. This means that there are about 14 hours of daylight in Buenos Aires, Cape Town and Adelaide, and only about 8 hours in London and Toronto.

July temperature

In July, it is summer in the northern hemisphere and winter in the southern hemisphere. It is warmer in the northern lands and colder in the south. The North Pole is tilted towards the sun. This means that in London and Toronto there are about 16 hours of daylight, but in Buenos Aires, Cape Town and Adelaide there are just under 10 hours.

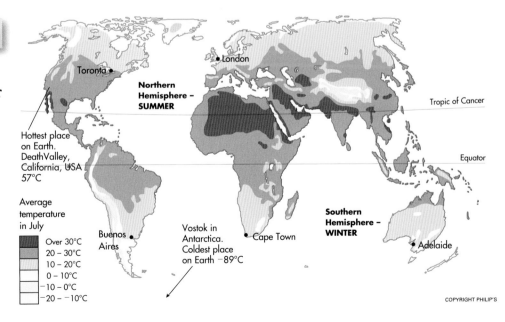

Toronto
London
Northern Hemisphere – SUMMER
Tropic of Cancer
Equator

Hottest place on Earth. Death Valley, California, USA 57°C

Average temperature in July
- Over 30°C
- 20 – 30°C
- 10 – 20°C
- 0 – 10°C
- −10 – 0°C
- −20 – −10°C

Buenos Aires
Vostok in Antarctica. Coldest place on Earth −89°C
Cape Town
Southern Hemisphere – WINTER
Adelaide

COPYRIGHT PHILIP'S

33

Climate change

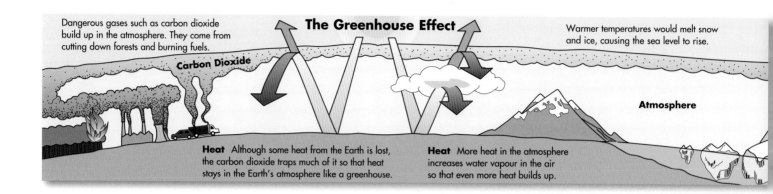

The Greenhouse Effect

Dangerous gases such as carbon dioxide build up in the atmosphere. They come from cutting down forests and burning fuels.

Carbon Dioxide

Warmer temperatures would melt snow and ice, causing the sea level to rise.

Atmosphere

Heat Although some heat from the Earth is lost, the carbon dioxide traps much of it so that heat stays in the Earth's atmosphere like a greenhouse.

Heat More heat in the atmosphere increases water vapour in the air so that even more heat builds up.

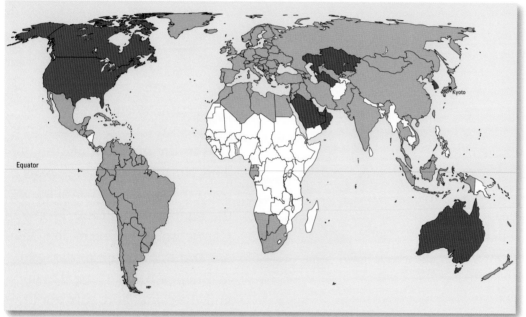

Equator

Kyoto

Carbon dioxide

Major producers of carbon dioxide

Other producers of carbon dioxide

Countries producing very little carbon dioxide

This map shows which countries produce the most carbon dioxide per person. The countries that contribute the most to global warming tend to be rich countries like the USA and Australia. Can you think of reasons why?

Global warming

Experts have studied climate data from all around the world. They agreed several years ago that climate change really was happening. Leaders of all the major countries in the world come together regularly to try and agree on what to do about it. This graph shows how temperatures might not rise as much if countries can cut their carbon dioxide emissions.

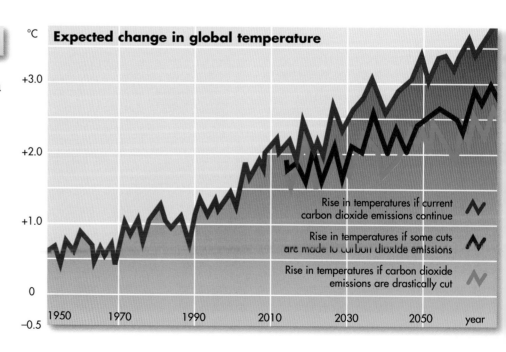

°C **Expected change in global temperature**

+3.0

+2.0

+1.0

0

−0.5

Rise in temperatures if current carbon dioxide emissions continue

Rise in temperatures if some cuts are made to carbon dioxide emissions

Rise in temperatures if carbon dioxide emissions are drastically cut

1950   1970   1990   2010   2030   2050   year

34

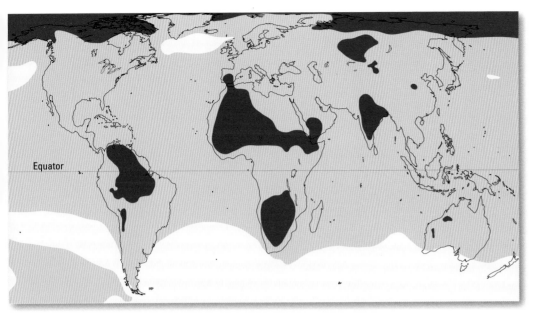

The expected change in temperature in the next 100 years

⬛	More than 5°C warmer
▨	Between 2°C and 5°C warmer
☐	Less than 2°C warmer

Compare this map with the map on the opposite page. The countries most affected by temperature change may not be the countries that are causing it.

Rainfall change

The expected change in the amount of rainfall in the next 100 years

▨	More rainfall
▨	Very little change in the amount of rainfall
☐	Less rainfall

As the global climate changes, some parts of the world will get more rainfall, while other parts will become drier. Can you think of the effects this might have?

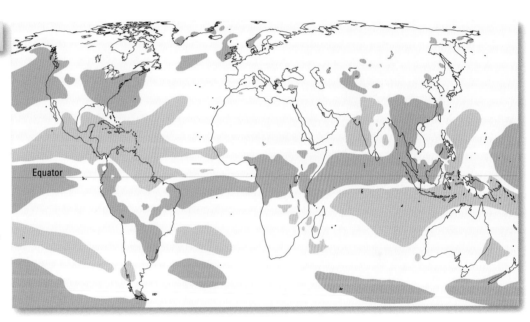

Sea level rise

Areas at risk from rising sea level

Areas with many low-lying islands

Warmer temperatures will result in ice caps melting in Antarctica and Greenland. Sea levels will rise and threaten low-lying coastal areas and islands. Many of the world's largest cities are threatened.

35

Forests, grasslands and wastes

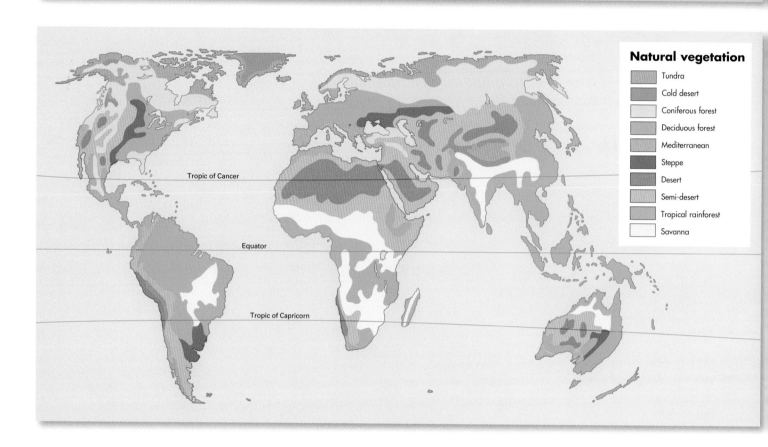

Natural vegetation
- Tundra
- Cold desert
- Coniferous forest
- Deciduous forest
- Mediterranean
- Steppe
- Desert
- Semi-desert
- Tropical rainforest
- Savanna

The map above shows types of vegetation. The diagram below shows the effect of altitude on types of vegetation.

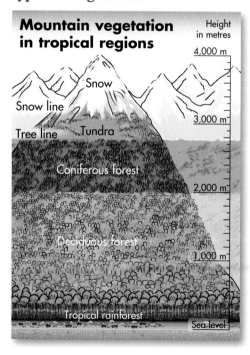

Mountain vegetation in tropical regions

Height in metres
- 4,000 m
- 3,000 m
- 2,000 m
- 1,000 m
- Sea level

Snow
Snow line
Tree line
Tundra
Coniferous forest
Deciduous forest
Tropical rainforest

Tundra
Long, dry, cold winters. Grasses, moss, bog and dwarf trees.

Coniferous forest
Harsh winters, mild summers. Trees have leaves all year.

Mediterranean
Hot, dry summers. Mild wet winters. Plants adapt to the heat.

Desert
Rain is rare. Plants only grow at oases with underground water.

Tropical rainforest (jungle)
Very hot and wet all the year. Tall trees and lush vegetation.

Cold desert
Very cold with little rain or snow. No plants can grow.

Deciduous forest
Rain all year, cool winters. Trees shed leaves in winter.

Steppe
Some rain with a dry season. Grasslands with some trees.

Semi-desert
Poor rains, sparse vegetation. Grass with a few small trees.

Savanna
Mainly dry, but lush grass grows when the rains come.

Tundra

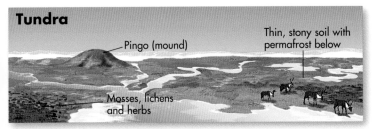

Pingo (mound)

Thin, stony soil with permafrost below

Mosses, lichens and herbs

Cold desert

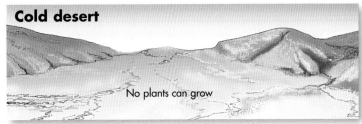

No plants can grow

Coniferous forest

Evergreen conifers (spruces and firs)

Young tree saplings and small shrubs

Carpet of pine needles

Ferns and brambles on edge of forest

Yearly cycle of a deciduous forest

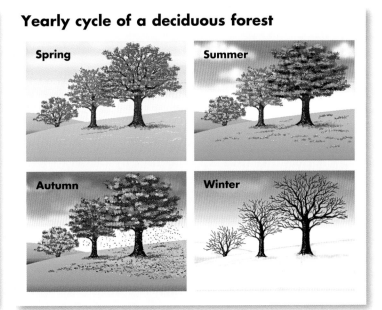

Spring

Summer

Autumn

Winter

Mediterranean

Small stunted trees

Scrub

Steppe

There are many plants in the steppe grasslands.

People planting crops can damage the natural habitat.

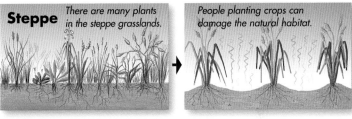

Tropical rainforest

Scattered trees with umbrella-shaped tops grow the highest.

Main layer of tall trees growing close together.

Creepers grow up the trees to reach the sunlight.

Ferns, mosses and small plants grow closest to the ground.

Desert

Palm trees

Sand blown into dunes by the wind

Cactus

Oasis

Semi-desert

Joshua trees

Grass and bush

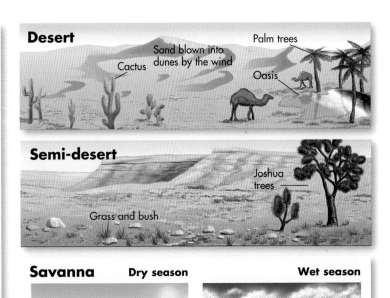

Savanna

Dry season

Wet season

Volcanoes and earthquakes

The Earth's crust is made up of a series of pieces called plates. The cracks between them are called plate boundaries. They are shown on the map below. In some areas the plates move towards each other and the heavier plate is forced under the lighter plate. If the plates rub together, the Earth's surface can be shaken backwards and forwards. Where the shaking is very destructive this is called an earthquake. Tsunami waves are caused by underwater earthquakes (see map opposite). When plates are forced down to great depths, they can melt to form magma. Volcanoes erupt when this magma is forced upwards to the surface.

Major volcanic eruptions since 1900

Year	Volcano	Deaths
1902	Mount Pelee, Martinique	29,025
1902	Soufriere, St. Vincent	1,680
1902	Santa Maria, Guatemala	6,000
1911	Taal, Philippines	1.335
1919	Kelud, Indonesia	5,110
1951	Mount Lamington, Papua New Guinea	2,942
1963	Agung, Indonesia	1,184
1982	El Chichon, Mexico	2,000
1985	Nevado del Ruiz, Colombia	25,000
1986	Lake Nyos, Cameroon	1,700
2018	Anak Krakatoa, Indonesia	437

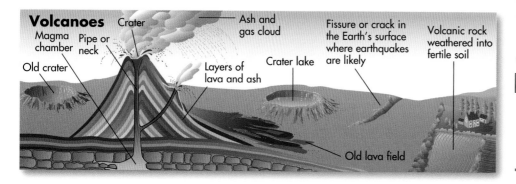

Volcanoes Crater — Ash and gas cloud — Fissure or crack in the Earth's surface where earthquakes are likely — Volcanic rock weathered into fertile soil
Magma chamber — Pipe or neck
Old crater — Crater lake
Layers of lava and ash
Old lava field

▨	Volcanic regions
△	Volcanoes (active since 1700)
1991	Year of major volcanic eruptions since 1900
——	Plate boundaries

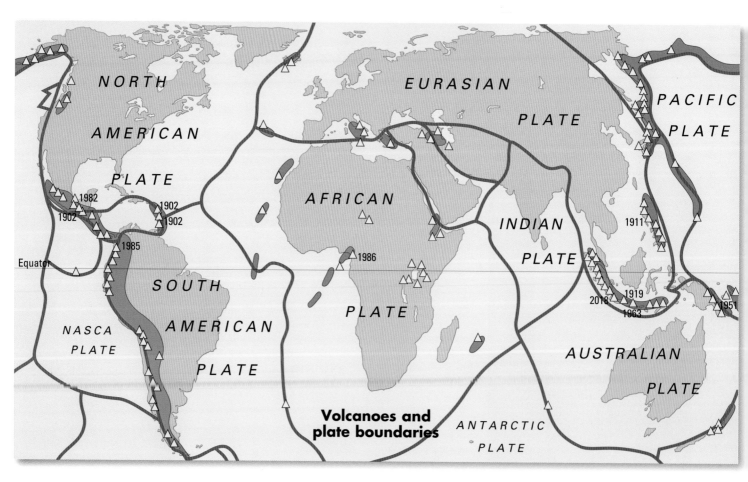

NORTH AMERICAN PLATE
EURASIAN PLATE
PACIFIC PLATE
AFRICAN PLATE
INDIAN PLATE
SOUTH AMERICAN PLATE
NASCA PLATE
AUSTRALIAN PLATE
ANTARCTIC PLATE
Equator
1982 1902 1902 1902 1985 1986 1911 1919 2018 1963 1951

Volcanoes and plate boundaries

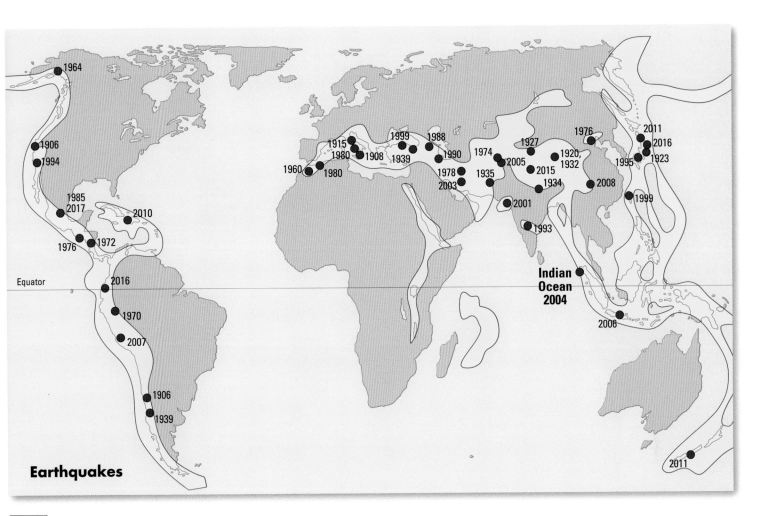

Earthquakes

Earthquake regions

• Major earthquakes since 1900 with dates

Major earthquakes since 1900

Year	Location	Magnitude	Deaths
1908	Messina, Italy	7.5	83,000
1915	Avezzano, Italy	7.5	30,000
1920	Gansu, China	8.6	180,000
1923	Yokohama, Japan	8.3	143,000
1927	Nan Shan, China	8.3	200,000
1932	Gansu, China	7.6	70,000
1970	Northern Peru	7.8	66,794
1976	Tangshan, China	8.2	255,000
1988	Armenia	6.8	55,000
1993	Maharashtra, India	6.4	30,000
2001	Gujarat, India	7.7	14,000
2003	Bam, Iran	7.1	30,000
2004	Sumatra, Indonesia	9.0	230,000
2005	Northern Pakistan	7.6	74,000
2008	Sichuan, China	7.9	70,000
2010	Haiti	7.0	230,000
2011	Northern Japan	9.0	22,600
2015	Central Nepal	7.8	8,500

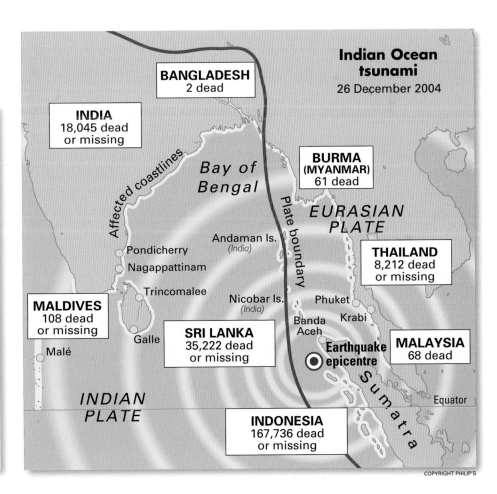

Indian Ocean tsunami 26 December 2004

COPYRIGHT PHILIP'S

Farming and fishing

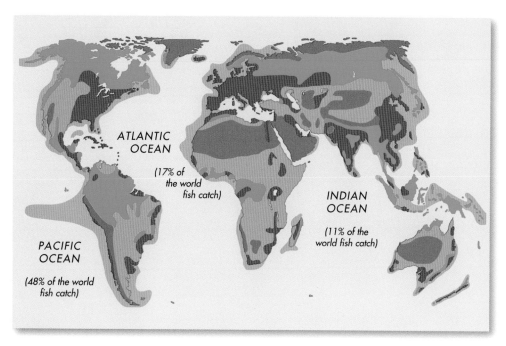

ATLANTIC OCEAN
(17% of the world fish catch)

INDIAN OCEAN
(11% of the world fish catch)

PACIFIC OCEAN
(48% of the world fish catch)

How the land is used

Forest areas with timber. Some hunting and fishing. Some farming in the tropics.

Deserts and wastelands

Animal farming on large farms (ranches)

Farming of crops and animals on large and small farms

Main fishing areas

Deserts and wastelands cover 32% of the world's total land area. Forests cover a further 30%. What percentage of the total land area does that leave for the farming of crops and animals?

The importance of agriculture

Over half the people work in agriculture

Between a quarter and half the people work in agriculture

Between one in ten and a quarter of the people work in agriculture

Less than one in ten of the people work in agriculture

A hundred years ago about 80% of the world's population worked in agriculture. Today it is only about 30% but agriculture is still very important in some countries.

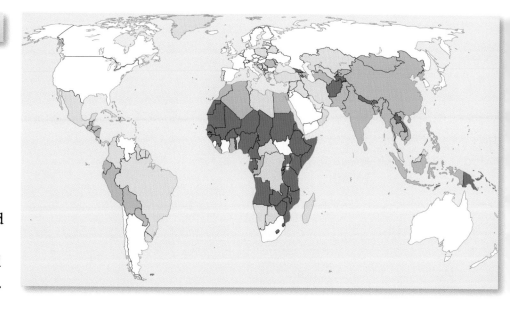

Methods of fishing

There are two types of sea fishing:

1. **Deep-sea fishing** using large trawlers which often stay at sea for many weeks.

2. **Inshore fishing** using small boats, traps and nets up to 70 km from the coast.

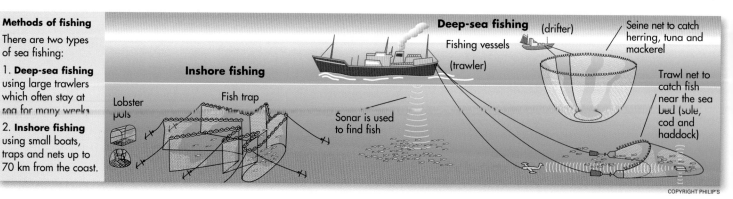

Inshore fishing

Lobster pots

Fish trap

Deep-sea fishing (drifter)

Fishing vessels (trawler)

Sonar is used to find fish

Seine net to catch herring, tuna and mackerel

Trawl net to catch fish near the sea bed (sole, cod and haddock)

COPYRIGHT PHILIP'S

Energy resources

Oil and gas resources

🛢 Oilfields

🌀 Natural gasfields

⟶ Main routes for transporting oil and gas by tanker

Crude oil is drilled from deep in the Earth's crust. The oil is then refined so that it can be used in different industries. Oil is used to make petrol and is also very important in the chemical industry. Natural gas is often found in the same places as oil.

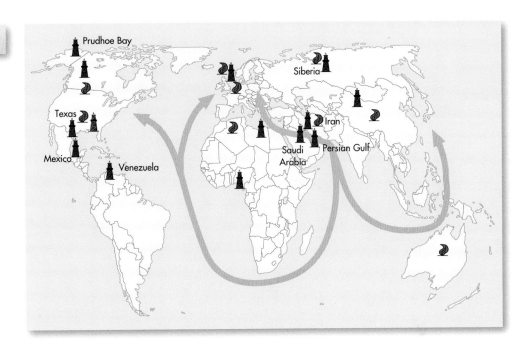

Coal resources

▲ Hard coal (bituminous)

▲ Lignite (soft brown coal)

⟶ Main routes for transporting coal

Coal is a fuel that comes from forests and swamps that rotted millions of years ago and have been crushed by layers of rock. The coal is cut out of the rock from deep mines and also from open-cast mines where the coal is nearer the surface. The oldest type of coal is hard. The coal formed more recently is softer.

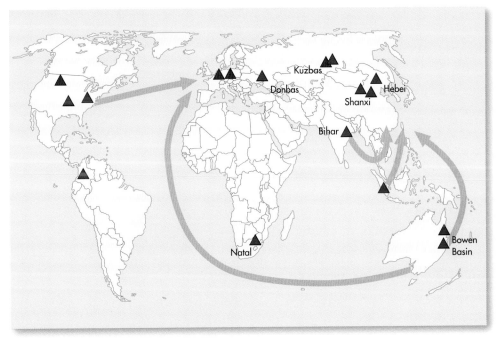

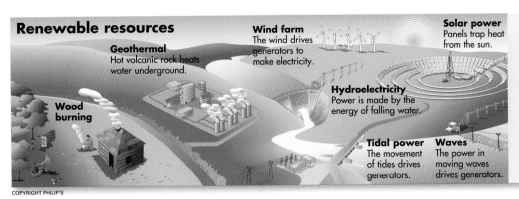

Renewable resources

Geothermal
Hot volcanic rock heats water underground.

Wood burning

Wind farm
The wind drives generators to make electricity.

Hydroelectricity
Power is made by the energy of falling water.

Solar power
Panels trap heat from the sun.

Tidal power
The movement of tides drives generators.

Waves
The power in moving waves drives generators.

Oil, gas and coal are all resources which provide energy. Once these resources have been used up, they cannot be replaced. They are called **non-renewable resources**.

Energy is also provided by the sun, wind, waves, tides, and hot water from deep in the Earth. These resources will never run out. They are called **renewable resources**.

Transport and tourism

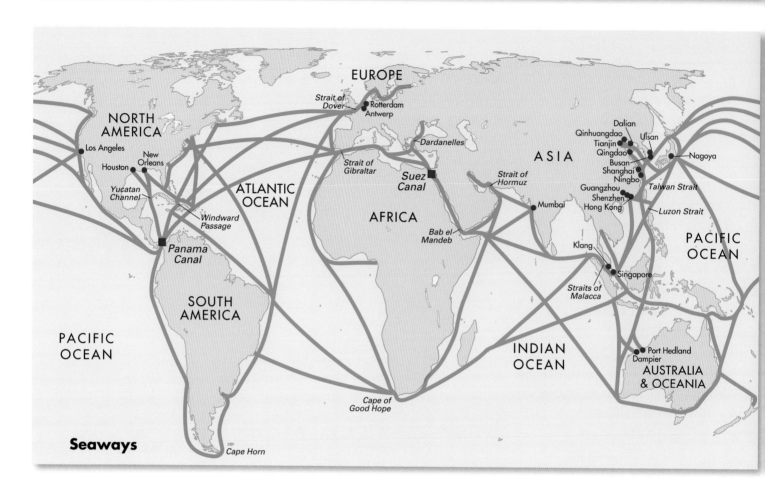

EUROPE

Strait of Dover

Rotterdam
Antwerp

NORTH AMERICA

Los Angeles

New Orleans

Houston

Yucatan Channel

Windward Passage

Panama Canal

ATLANTIC OCEAN

Dardanelles

Strait of Gibraltar

Suez Canal

AFRICA

Bab el Mandeb

Strait of Hormuz

Mumbai

ASIA

Dalian
Qinhuangdao
Tianjin   Ulsan
Qingdao
Busan
Shanghai
Ningbo
Guangzhou
Shenzhen
Hong Kong

Nagoya

Taiwan Strait

Luzon Strait

PACIFIC OCEAN

Klang

SOUTH AMERICA

PACIFIC OCEAN

INDIAN OCEAN

Straits of Malacca

Singapore

Port Hedland
Dampier

AUSTRALIA & OCEANIA

Cape of Good Hope

Seaways

Cape Horn

—— Main shipping routes

● The biggest seaports in the world

Sea transport is used for goods that are too bulky or heavy to go by air or land. The main shipping routes are between North America, Europe and the Far East.

CARIBBEAN SEA

Colon

Locks

Lake Gatun (26 metres above sea level)

PANAMA

Gaillard Cut

Panama Canal

Locks

Panama

PACIFIC OCEAN

Los Angeles

Rotterdam

14,800 km

Panama Canal

25,200 km

PACIFIC OCEAN

ATLANTIC OCEAN

Cape Horn

Panama Canal

- Opened in 1914
- 82 km long
- 13,000 ships a year
- Average toll $54,000
- Locks are needed in the Panama Canal to go between the Caribbean Sea and the Pacific Ocean

Panama Canal and Suez Canal

These two important canals cut through narrow pieces of land. Can you work out how much shorter the journeys are by using the canals?

Suez Canal

- Opened in 1870
- 162 km long
- 21,000 ships a year
- Average toll $250,000
- The Suez Canal has no locks between the Mediterranean Sea and the Red Sea

Rotterdam

Suez Canal

Mumbai

10,000 km

17,400 km

ATLANTIC OCEAN

INDIAN OCEAN

Cape of Good Hope

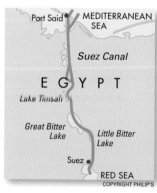

Port Said

MEDITERRANEAN SEA

Suez Canal

EGYPT

Lake Timsah

Great Bitter Lake

Little Bitter Lake

Suez

RED SEA

COPYRIGHT PHILIP'S

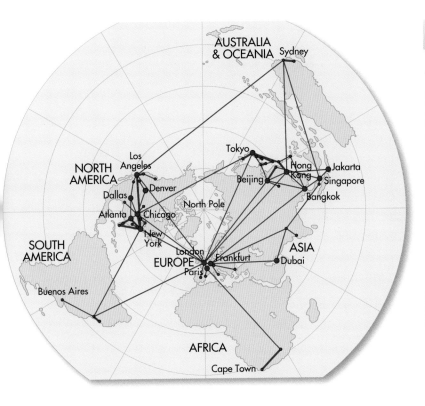

Airways

This map has the North Pole at its centre. It shows how much air traffic connects Europe, North America and Eastern Asia. You can see the long distances in the USA and Asia that are covered by air.

- ● Large international airports (over 50 million passengers a year)
- · Other important airports
- ▬ Heavily used air routes
- — Other important air routes

Tourism

In 2019 there were 1,500 million tourists visiting foreign countries. The most popular country to visit was France, followed by Spain, the USA, China.

- ☐ Ski resorts
- ▨ Centres of entertainment
- ■ Cultural and historical centres
- ▨ Places of pilgrimage
- ▨ Places of great natural beauty
- ☐ Coastal resorts

Air distances (kilometres)

	Buenos Aires	Cape Town	London	Los Angeles	New York	Sydney	Tokyo
Buenos Aires		6,880	11,128	9,854	8,526	11,760	18,338
Cape Town	6,880		9,672	16,067	12,551	10,982	14,710
London	11,128	9,672		8,752	5,535	17,005	9,584
Los Angeles	9,854	16,067	8,752		3,968	12,052	8,806
New York	8,526	12,551	5,535	3,968		16,001	10,869
Sydney	11,760	10,982	17,005	12,052	16,001		7,809
Tokyo	18,338	14,710	9,584	8,806	10,869	7,809	

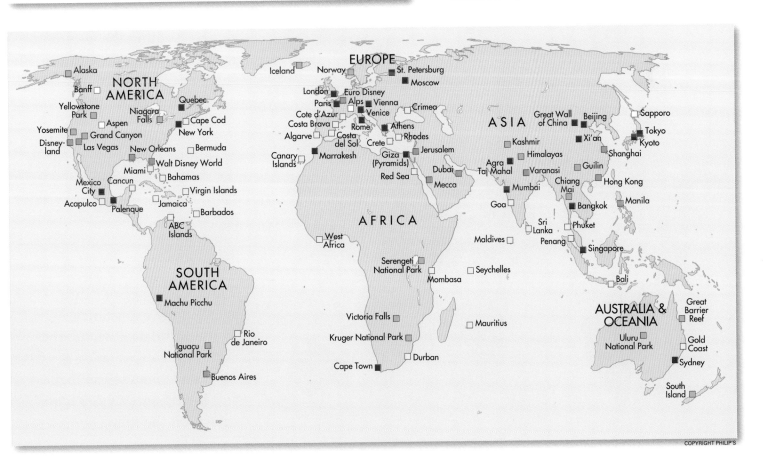

43

Rich and poor

All countries have both rich and poor people but some countries have more poor people than others. The amount of food that people have to eat and the age that they die can often depend on where they live in the world. The world can be divided into two parts – the rich and the poor.

The rich countries are mostly in the North and the poor countries are mostly in the South. The map below shows which countries are rich and which are poor. The list on the right shows some contrasts between rich and poor. Some of these contrasts can be seen in the maps on these pages.

Rich
- Good health
- Well educated
- Well fed
- Small families
- Many industries
- Few farmers
- Give aid

Poor
- Poor health
- Poorly educated
- Poorly fed
- Large families
- Few industries
- Many farmers
- Receive aid

Poor countries have over three-quarters of the world's population but less than a quarter of its wealth.

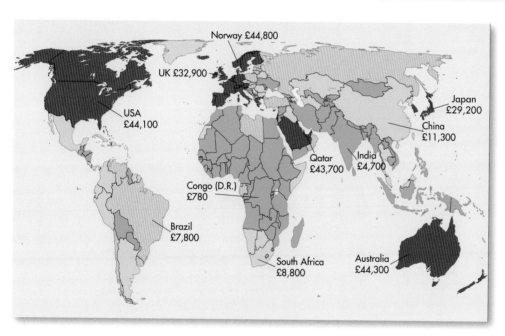

Income

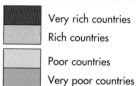

- Very rich countries
- Rich countries
- Poor countries
- Very poor countries

The map shows how much money there is to spend on each person in a country. This is called income per person – this is worked out by dividing the wealth of a country by its population. The map gives examples of rich and poor countries.

How long do people live?

This is the average age when people die

- Over 75 years
- 60 – 75 years
- Under 60 years

The average age of death is called life expectancy. In the world as a whole, the average life expectancy is 71 years. Some of the highest and lowest ages of death are shown on the map.

Food and famine

Below the amount of food they need

Above the amount of food they need

Over a third above the amount of food they need

★ Major famines since 1980

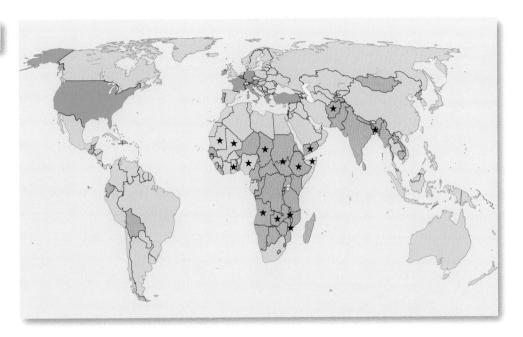

If people do not have enough to eat they become unhealthy. This map shows where in the world people have less than and more than the amount of food they need to live a healthy life.

Reading and writing

Over half the adults cannot read or write

Between a quarter and a half of the adults cannot read or write

Less than a quarter of the adults cannot read or write

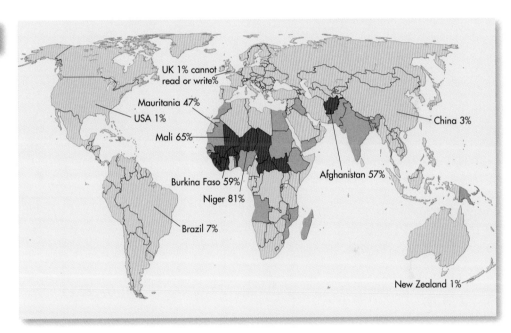

UK 1% cannot read or write%

Mauritania 47%

USA 1%

Mali 65%

China 3%

Burkina Faso 59%

Afghanistan 57%

Niger 81%

Brazil 7%

New Zealand 1%

The map shows the proportion of adults in each country who cannot read or write a simple sentence. Can you think of some reasons why more people cannot read or write in some places in the world than in others?

Development aid

Over £25 received per person each year

Up to £25 received per person each year

Up to £100 given per person each year

Over £100 given per person each year

Countries that receive or give no aid

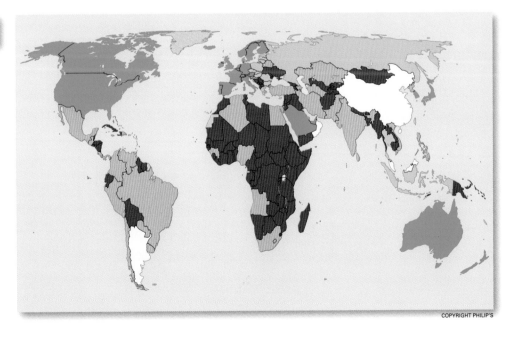

Some countries receive aid from other countries. Money is one type of aid. It is used to help with food, health and education problems. The map shows how much different countries give or receive.

Peoples and cities

Where people live

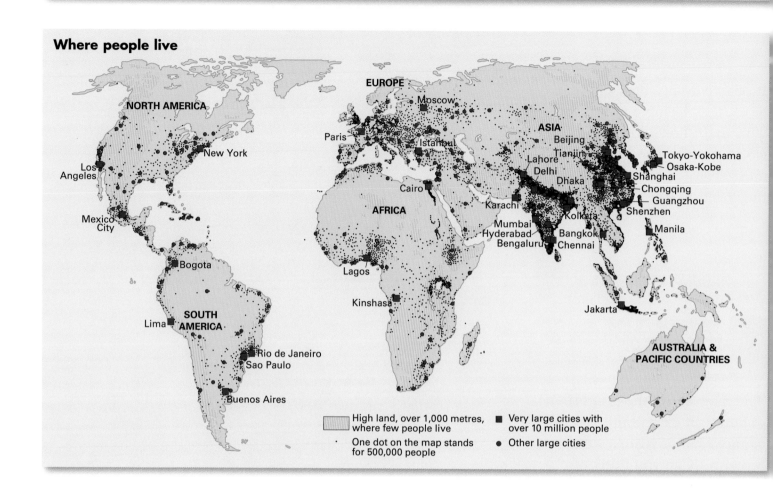

High land, over 1,000 metres, where few people live

One dot on the map stands for 500,000 people

Very large cities with over 10 million people

Other large cities

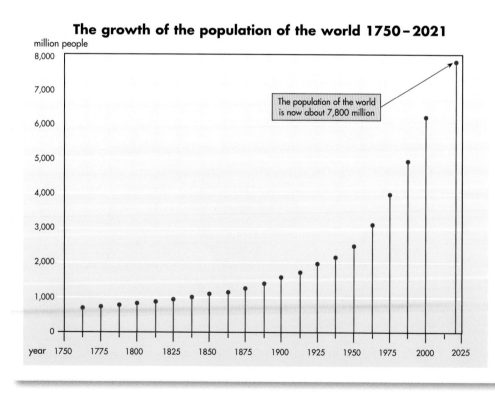

The growth of the population of the world 1750–2021

million people

The population of the world is now about 7,800 million

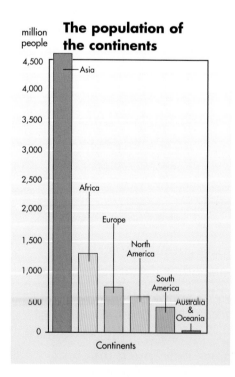

The population of the continents

million people

Largest nations

(population of countries in millions)

1. China 1,398
2. India 1,339
3. USA 335
4. Indonesia. 275
5. Pakistan. 238
6. Nigeria 220
7. Brazil. 213
8. Bangladesh 164
9. Russia 142
10. Mexico 130
11. Japan. 125
12. Ethiopia. 111
13. Philippines. 111
14. Egypt. 106
15. Congo (Dem. Rep.) 105
16. Vietnam. 103
17 . Iran 86
16. Turkey 83
17. Germany 80
20. Thailand 70
21. France. 68
22. UK 66

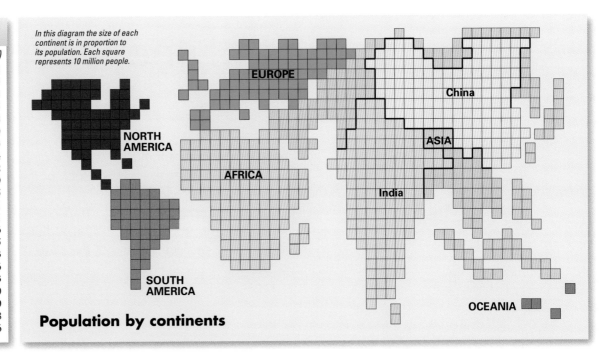

In this diagram the size of each continent is in proportion to its population. Each square represents 10 million people.

Population by continents

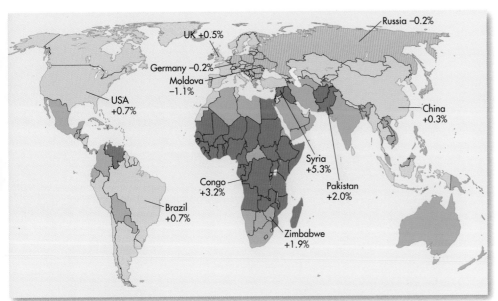

Increase and decrease

Annual rate of change in 2021

- Over 2% gain in the number of people
- Between 1% and 2% gain
- Under 1% gain
- Loss in the number of people

The map shows the rate of change in the number of people in each country. The largest increases are in poor countries in Africa and Asia. The number of people living in some richer countries is decreasing.

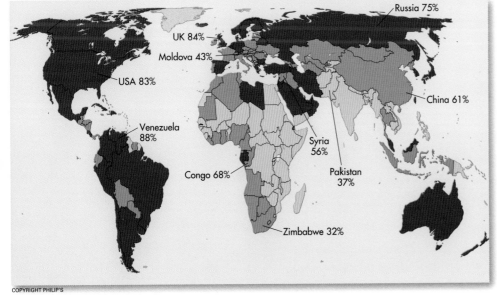

Living in cities

Urban population as a percentage of the total population in 2021

- Over three-quarters of the population live in cities
- Between a half and three-quarters live in cities
- Less than half live in cities

In 2008, for the first time in history, more than half of the world's population lived in cities. Why do you think people move from farms and villages to towns and cities?

Countries of the world

North America

(see pages 58–59)

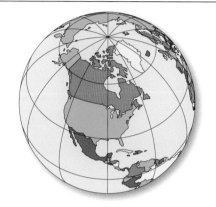

These pages show different maps of the world. The large map shows the world cut through the Pacific Ocean and opened out on to flat paper. The smaller maps of the continents are views of the globe looking down on each of the continents.

Larger maps of the continents appear on the following pages. They show more cities than on this map.

South America

(see pages 60–61)

Africa

(see pages 54–55)

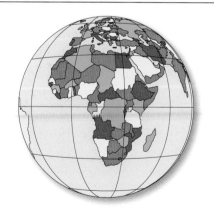

■ Cities with more than 10 million people

Europe

(see pages 50–51)

Asia

(see pages 52–53)

Oceania

(see pages 56–57)

GREENLAND
(Denmark)

Arctic Circle

ICELAND

Svalbard
(Norway)

RUSSIA

UNITED
KINGDOM

DENMARK

NORWAY
SWEDEN
FINLAND
ESTONIA
LATVIA
LITHUANIA
BELARUS

Moscow

IRELAND

NETH.
GERMANY POLAND
BELG. LUX. CZECH.
SLOVAKIA UKRAINE
AUSTRIA HUNGARY MOLDOVA
SWITZ. SLO. ROMANIA

KAZAKHSTAN

MONGOLIA

Paris
FRANCE

ITALY

B.-H.
S. M. BULGARIA
ALB. N.M.

Istanbul

GEORGIA

UZBEKISTAN

KYRGYZSTAN

Beijing
Tianjin

NORTH
KOREA

JAPAN
Tokyo

PORTUGAL SPAIN

GREECE

TURKEY

AZER.

ARM.

CHINA

SOUTH
KOREA

Azores
(Portugal)

CYPRUS
LEB.
ISRAEL
JORDAN

SYRIA

TURKMENISTAN

AFGHANISTAN
TAJIKISTAN

Shanghai
Chongqing

PACIFIC

MOROCCO

TUNISIA

IRAQ

IRAN

Lahore
Delhi

PAKISTAN

NEPAL

BHUTAN

Guangzhou

TAIWAN

Tropic of Cancer

Cairo

KUWAIT

Canary Islands
(Spain)

ALGERIA

LIBYA

EGYPT

BAHRAIN
QATAR
U.A.E.

Karachi

BANGLA-
DESH

Kolkata

Dhaka

Shenzhen

OCEAN

WESTERN
SAHARA

SAUDI
ARABIA

OMAN

INDIA

MYANMAR
(Burma)

NORTHERN
MARIANAS

MAURITANIA

MALI

NIGER

CHAD

SUDAN

ERITREA

YEMEN

Mumbai
Hyderabad

LAOS
THAI-
LAND

Manila

PHILIPPINES

Guam
(U.S.A.)

SENEGAL
GAMBIA
GUINEA
BISSAU

BURKINA
FASO

DJIBOUTI

Bengaluru

Chennai

Bangkok

CAMBODIA

MARSHALL
ISLANDS

GUINEA
SIERRA
LEONE
LIBERIA

COTE
D'IVOIRE

GHANA

NIGERIA

Lagos

CENTRAL
AFRICAN
REP.

SOUTH
SUDAN

ETHIOPIA

SRI
LANKA

VIETNAM

PALAU

FEDERATED STATES
OF MICRONESIA

CAMEROON

SOMALIA

MALDIVES

BRUNEI

MALAYSIA

EQUATORIAL
GUINEA

UGANDA

KENYA

SINGAPORE

Equator

GABON

CONGO

Democratic
Republic
of the
CONGO

RWANDA
BURUNDI

Borneo

INDONESIA

New
Guinea

PAPUA
NEW
GUINEA

SOLOMON
ISLANDS

KIRIBATI

Ascencion
(U.K.)

CABINDA

Kinshasa

TANZANIA

SEYCHELLES

INDIAN

Jakarta

Sumatra

TIMOR-LESTE

TUVALU

ANGOLA

MALAWI

ZAMBIA

COMOROS

Cocos Islands
(Australia)

Christmas
Island
(Australia)

St. Helena
(U.K.)

ZIMBABWE

MOZAMBIQUE

MADAGASCAR

OCEAN

VANUATU

FIJI

MAURITIUS

ATLANTIC

NAMIBIA

BOTSWANA

Réunion
(France)

New
Caledonia
(France)

Tropic of Capricorn

OCEAN

SOUTH
AFRICA

ESWATINI

LESOTHO

AUSTRALIA

Tristan da
Cunha
(U.K.)

Prince Edward
Islands
(South Africa)

Crozet Islands
(France)

Kerguelen Islands
(France)

NEW
ZEALAND

South Georgia
(U.K.)

SOUTHERN OCEAN

West from Greenwich

ANTARCTICA

East from Greenwich

Antarctic Circle

COPYRIGHT PHILIP'S

ALB.	= Albania	LUX.	= Luxembourg
ARM.	= Armenia	M.	= Montenegro
AZER.	= Azerbaijan	NETH.	= Netherlands
BELG.	= Belgium	N.M.	= North Macedonia
B.-H.	= Bosnia-Herzegovina	S.	= Serbia
CR.	= Croatia	SLO.	= Slovenia
CZECH.	= Czechia	SWITZ.	= Switzerland
DOM. REP	= Dominican Republic	U.A.E.	= United Arab Emirates
K.	= Kosovo	U.K.	= United Kingdom
LEB.	= Lebanon	U.S.A.	= United States of America

Europe

Largest countries – by area
(thousand square kilometres)

1. Russia 17,075
2. Ukraine 604
3. France 552
4. Spain 498

Largest countries – by population
(million people)

1. Russia. 142
2. Germany 80
3. France 68
4. United Kingdom 66

Largest cities
(million people)

1. Istanbul (TURKEY) 15.2
2. Moscow (RUSSIA) 12.5
3. Paris (FRANCE) 11.0
4. London (UK) 9.3

- *Europe is the second smallest continent. It is one-fifth the size of Asia. Australia is slightly smaller than Europe.*
- *The Ural Mountains form the eastern boundary of Europe.*
- *Great Britain is the largest island in Europe.*

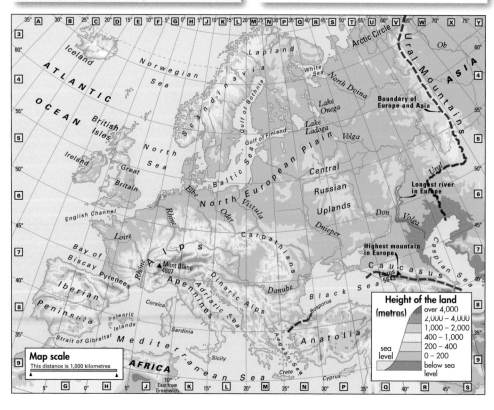

Map scale
This distance is 1,000 kilometres

Height of the land (metres)
- over 4,000
- 2,000 – 4,000
- 1,000 – 2,000
- 400 – 1,000
- 200 – 400
- sea level 0 – 200
- below sea level

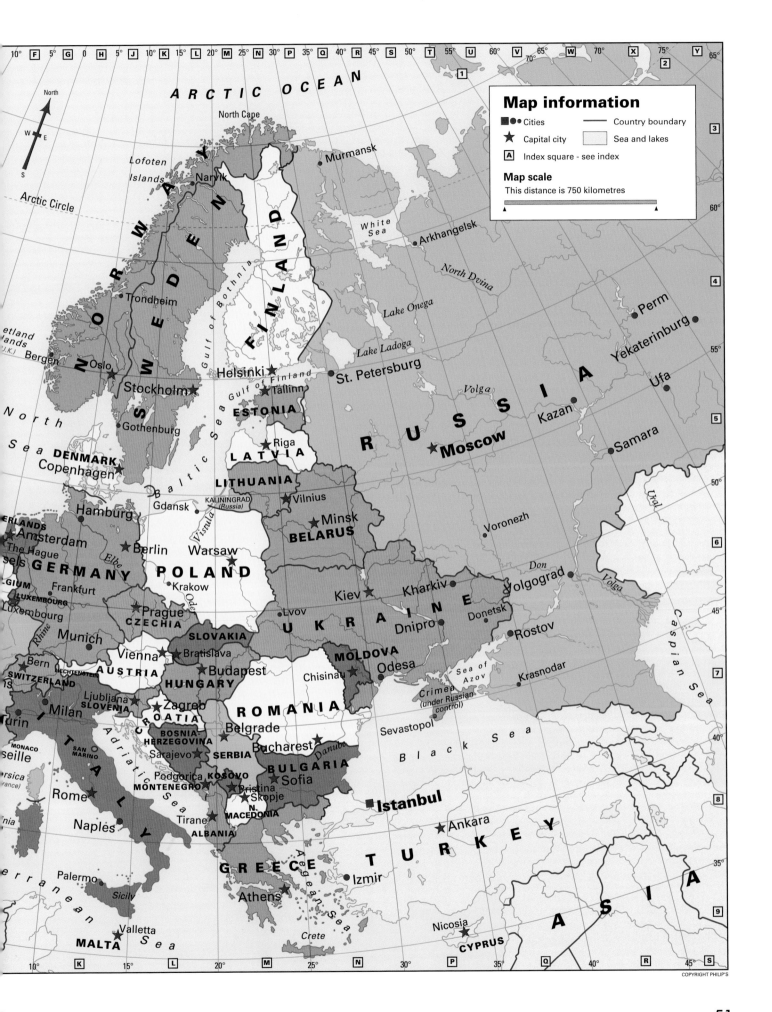

ARCTIC OCEAN

North Cape

North

W E

S

Arctic Circle

Lofoten
Islands

Narvik

Murmansk

Map information

■●● Cities   —— Country boundary

★ Capital city   Sea and lakes

Ⓐ Index square - see index

Map scale

This distance is 750 kilometres

▲   ▲

Trondheim

N
O
R
W
A
Y

S
W
E
D
E
N

F
I
N
L
A
N
D

White
Sea

Arkhangelsk

North Divina

Lake Onega

Lake Ladoga

etland
lands
(U.K.)

Bergen

Oslo

Stockholm

Gulf of Bothnia

Helsinki

Gulf of Finland

Tallinn

ESTONIA

St. Petersburg

R   U   S   S   I   A

Volga

Perm

Yekaterinburg

Ufa

Gothenburg

Riga

LATVIA

Baltic Sea

Kazan

★ **Moscow**

Samara

DENMARK

Copenhagen

LITHUANIA

Gdansk

KALININGRAD
(Russia)

Vilnius

Ural

North
Sea

Hamburg

Berlin

Warsaw

Vistula

Minsk

BELARUS

Voronezh

ERLANDS

Amsterdam

The Hague

els

GERMANY

Elbe

Oder

Prague

Frankfurt

POLAND

Krakow

Kiev

Kharkiv

Volgograd

Don

Volga

GIUM

LUXEMBOURG

Luxembourg

CZECHIA

Lvov

U   K   R   A   I   N   E

Dnipro

Donetsk

Rostov

Rhine

Munich

SLOVAKIA

Bratislava

MOLDOVA

Krasnodar

Caspian Sea

Bern

Vienna

LIECHTENSTEIN

AUSTRIA

HUNGARY

Budapest

Chisinau

Odesa

Sea of
Azov

SWITZERLAND

IS

Ljubljana

SLOVENIA

Zagreb

CROATIA

ROMANIA

Crimea
(under Russian
control)

Milan

Turin

**BOSNIA-
HERZEGOVINA**

Belgrade

Sevastopol

Black   Sea

MONACO

SAN
MARINO

Sarajevo

SERBIA

Bucharest

Danube

seille

Podgorica

KOSOVO

BULGARIA

Sofia

orsica
rance)

I
T
A
L
Y

Adriatic
Sea

MONTENEGRO

Pristina

Skopje

Rome

**N.
MACEDONIA**

Istanbul

Ankara

T   U   R   K   E   Y

A
S
I
A

Naples

Tirane

ALBANIA

inia

GREECE

Aegean
Sea

Izmir

rranean

Palermo

Sicily

Athens

Black Sea

Nicosia

A   S   I   A

Valletta

Crete

Sea

MALTA

CYPRUS

COPYRIGHT PHILIP'S

51

Asia

Largest countries – by area
(thousand square kilometres)

1. Russia 17,075
2. China 9,597
3. India 3,287

Largest countries – by population
(million people)

1. China 1,398
2. India 1,339
3. Indonesia 275
4. Pakistan 238

Largest cities
(million people)

1. Tokyo (JAPAN) 37.4
2. Delhi (INDIA) 30.3
3. Shanghai (CHINA) 27.1
4. Dhaka (BANGLADESH) . . 21.0
5. Beijing (CHINA) 20.5

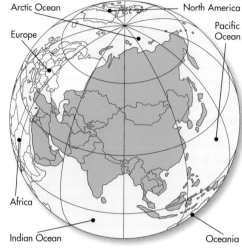

- Asia is the largest continent. It is twice the size of North America.
- It is a continent of long rivers. Many of Asia's rivers are longer than Europe's longest river.
- Asia contains well over half of the world's population.

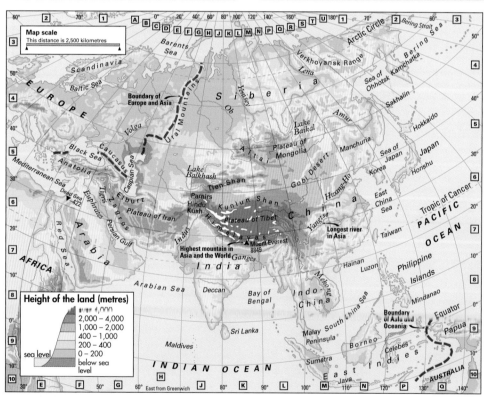

Map information

- ■●● Cities
- ★ Capital city
- Ⓐ Index square - see index
- —— Country boundary
- ▭ Sea and lakes

Map scale
This distance is 2,000 kilometres

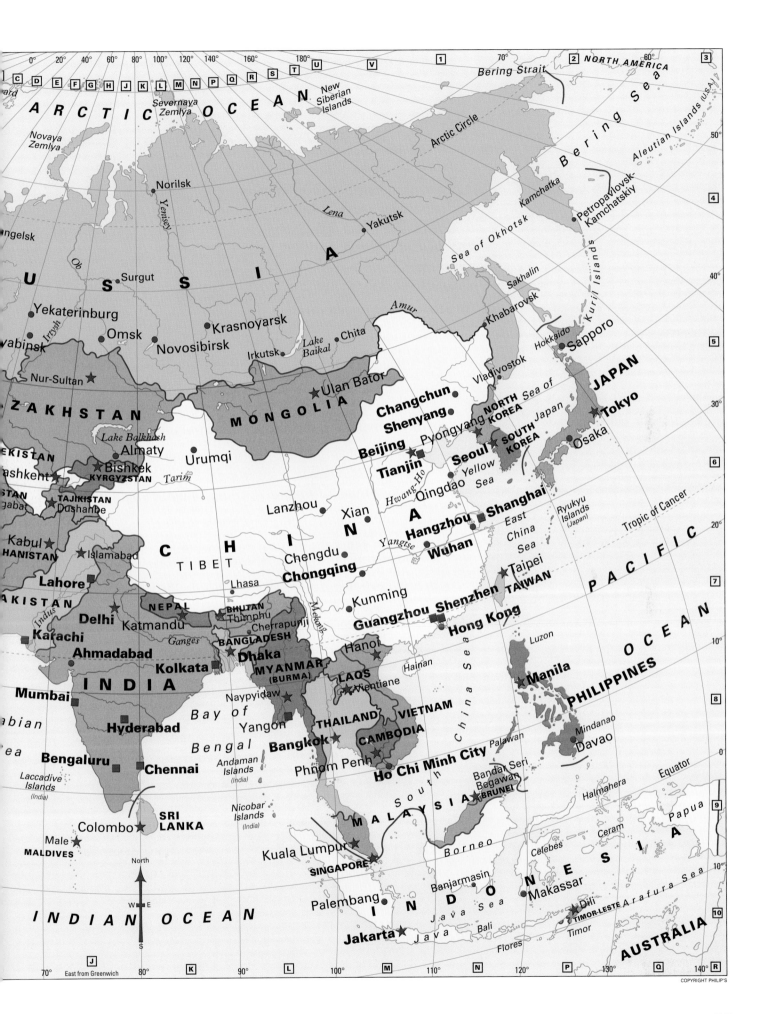

ARCTIC OCEAN

Novaya
Zemlya
Severnaya
Zemlya
New
Siberian
Islands
Bering Strait NORTH AMERICA

Bering
Sea

Norilsk

Arctic Circle

Aleutian Islands (U.S.A)

Yenisey
Lena
Yakutsk

Kamchatka

Sea of Okhotsk
Petropavlovsk-
Kamchatskiy

ngelsk

R U S S I A

Surgut

Yekaterinburg

Krasnoyarsk
Chita
Khabarovsk

Kuril Islands

vabinsk
Omsk
Novosibirsk
Irkutsk
Lake
Baikal
Amur
Sakhalin

Hokkaido
Sapporo

JAPAN

Irtysh
Ob

Nur-Sultan

Ulan Bator

Vladivostok
Sea of
Japan

Tokyo

ZAKHSTAN

MONGOLIA

Changchun
Shenyang
NORTH
KOREA

Osaka

Lake Balkhash
Almaty

Urumqi

Beijing
Pyongyang
SOUTH
KOREA
Seoul

EKISTAN
Bishkek
KYRGYZSTAN
Tarim
Tianjin
Yellow
Qingdao
Sea

Ryukyu
Islands
(Japan)
Tropic of Cancer

ashkent

TAJIKISTAN
Dushanbe
Lanzhou
Xian
Hwang-Ho
C H I N A
Hangzhou
Shanghai
East
China
Sea

gabat

Kabul
HANISTAN
Islamabad
C
TIBET
Chengdu
Chongqing
Yangtse
Wuhan

Taipei

PACIFIC

Lahore
Lhasa
Kunming
TAIWAN

AKISTAN
Indus
NEPAL
Katmandu
BHUTAN
Thimphu
Cherrapunji
Mekong
Guangzhou
Shenzhen
Hong Kong

OCEAN

Delhi
Ganges
BANGLADESH

Luzon

Karachi
Dhaka
Hanoi

Ahmadabad
Kolkata
MYANMAR
(BURMA)
LAOS
Hainan

Manila
PHILIPPINES

I N D I A
Naypyidaw
Vientiane

Mumbai
Bay of
Yangon
THAILAND
VIETNAM

China Sea

Hyderabad
Bengal
Bangkok
CAMBODIA

Mindanao
Davao

abian
Andaman
Islands
(India)
Phnom Penh
Ho Chi Minh City
Palawan

Bengaluru
Chennai
Equator

Sea
Laccadive
Islands
(India)
SRI
LANKA
Nicobar
Islands
(India)
Bandar Seri
Begawan
BRUNEI
Halmahera
Papua

Colombo
South

Male
MALDIVES
North
M A L A Y S I A
Borneo
Celebes
Ceram
N E S I A

Kuala Lumpur
SINGAPORE
Banjarmasin
Makassar

INDIAN OCEAN
W   E
S
Palembang
I N D O
Java Sea
Dili
TIMOR-LESTE Arafura Sea

Jakarta
Java
Bali
Flores
Timor
AUSTRALIA

Africa

- Africa is the second largest continent. Asia is the largest.

- There are over 50 countries, some of them small in area and population. The population of Africa is growing more quickly than any other continent.

- Parts of Africa have a dry, desert climate. Other parts are tropical.

- The highest mountains run from north to south on the eastern side of Africa. The Great Rift Valley is a volcanic valley that was formed 10 to 20 million years ago by a crack in the Earth's crust. Mount Kenya and Kilimanjaro are examples of old volcanoes in the area.

- The Sahara is the largest desert in the world.

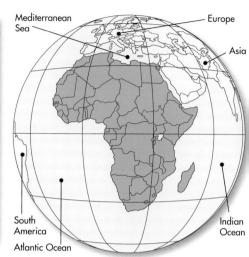

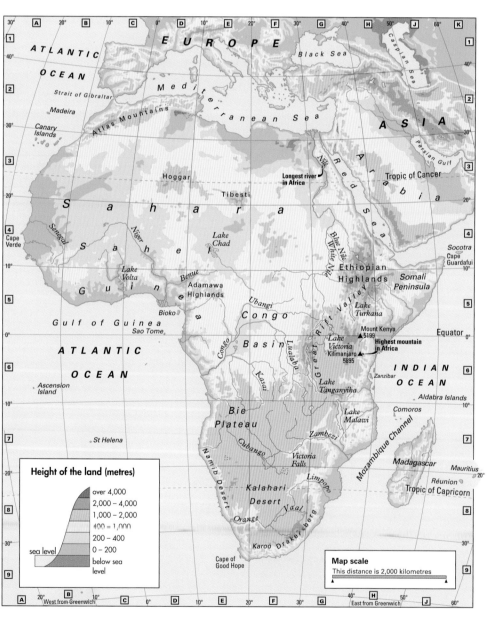

Largest countries – by area

(thousand square kilometres)

1. Algeria 2,382
2. Congo (Dem. Rep.) . . 2,345
3. Sudan. 1,886
4. Libya 1,760
5. Chad 1,284
6. Niger 1,267

Largest countries – by population

(million people)

1. Nigeria 220
2. Ethiopia 111
3. Egypt 106
4. Congo (Dem. Rep.) 105
5. Tanzania 62
6. South Africa 57

Largest cities

(million people)

1. Cairo (EGYPT) 20.9
2. Lagos (NIGERIA) 14.4
3. Kinshasa (CONGO, D. R.) . 14.3
4. Luanda (ANGOLA) 8.3
5. Dar es Salaam (TANZANIA) 6.7

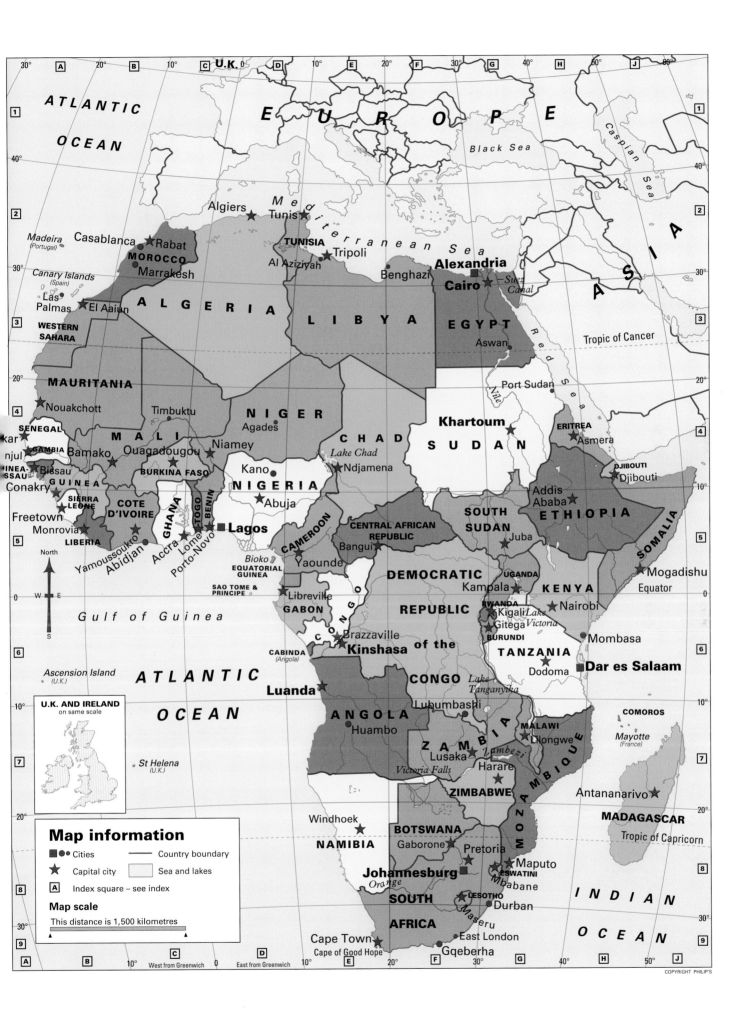

ATLANTIC OCEAN

EUROPE

Black Sea

Caspian Sea

ASIA

Mediterranean Sea

Algiers
Tunis
TUNISIA
Casablanca
Madeira (Portugal)
Rabat
MOROCCO
Marrakesh
Tripoli
Al Aziziyah
Benghazi
Alexandria
Cairo
Suez Canal

Canary Islands (Spain)
Las Palmas
El Aaiun
WESTERN SAHARA

A L G E R I A

L I B Y A

EGYPT
Aswan

Tropic of Cancer

Red Sea
Nile
Port Sudan

MAURITANIA
Nouakchott
Timbuktu
N I G E R
Agades
Niamey

Khartoum
S U D A N

ERITREA
Asmera

SENEGAL
kar
njul
GAMBIA
Bamako
M A L I
Ouagadougou
BURKINA FASO
INEA-SSAU
Bissau
GUINEA
Conakry
SIERRA LEONE
Freetown
Monrovia
LIBERIA
Yamoussoukro
Abidjan
Accra
COTE D'IVOIRE
GHANA
TOGO
BENIN
Lome
Porto-Novo
Kano
N I G E R I A
Abuja
Lagos
L A K E   C H A D
Lake Chad
Ndjamena
C H A D

DJIBOUTI
Djibouti
Addis Ababa
ETHIOPIA

SOMALIA

Bioko
EQUATORIAL GUINEA
SAO TOME & PRINCIPE
Libreville
GABON
Yaounde
CAMEROON
Bangui
CENTRAL AFRICAN REPUBLIC

SOUTH SUDAN
Juba

Mogadishu
Equator

DEMOCRATIC
REPUBLIC
of the
CONGO
Kinshasa
Brazzaville
CONGO
CABINDA (Angola)

UGANDA
Kampala
RWANDA
Kigali
BURUNDI
Gitega
Lake Victoria
Nairobi
K E N Y A
Mombasa

TANZANIA
Dodoma
Dar es Salaam
Lake Tanganyika

COMOROS
Mayotte (France)

Luanda
A N G O L A
Huambo
Lubumbashi

ATLANTIC
OCEAN
Ascension Island (U.K.)
St Helena (U.K.)

ZAMBIA
Lusaka
Zambezi
Victoria Falls
Harare
MALAWI
Lilongwe
MOZAMBIQUE

Antananarivo
MADAGASCAR
Tropic of Capricorn

ZIMBABWE
Windhoek
BOTSWANA
Gaborone
NAMIBIA
Pretoria
Maputo
ESWATINI
Mbabane
Johannesburg
Orange
LESOTHO
Maseru
Durban
SOUTH
AFRICA
East London
Cape Town
Cape of Good Hope
Gqeberha

INDIAN
OCEAN

North
W E
S

Gulf of Guinea

U.K. AND IRELAND
on same scale

Map information
■●● Cities
⭐ Capital city
Ⓐ Index square – see index

— Country boundary
Sea and lakes

Map scale
This distance is 1,500 kilometres

West from Greenwich | East from Greenwich

COPYRIGHT PHILIP'S

55

Australia and Oceania

■ *The continent is often called Oceania. It is made up of the huge island of Australia and thousands of smaller islands in the Pacific Ocean.*

■ *It is the smallest continent, only about a sixth the size of Asia.*

■ *The highest mountain is on the Indonesian part of New Guinea which many consider to be part of Asia.*

Largest countries – by area
(thousand square kilometres)

1. Australia 7,741
2. Papua New Guinea . . . 463
3. New Zealand 271

Largest countries – by population
(million people)

1. Australia 26
2. Papua New Guinea 7

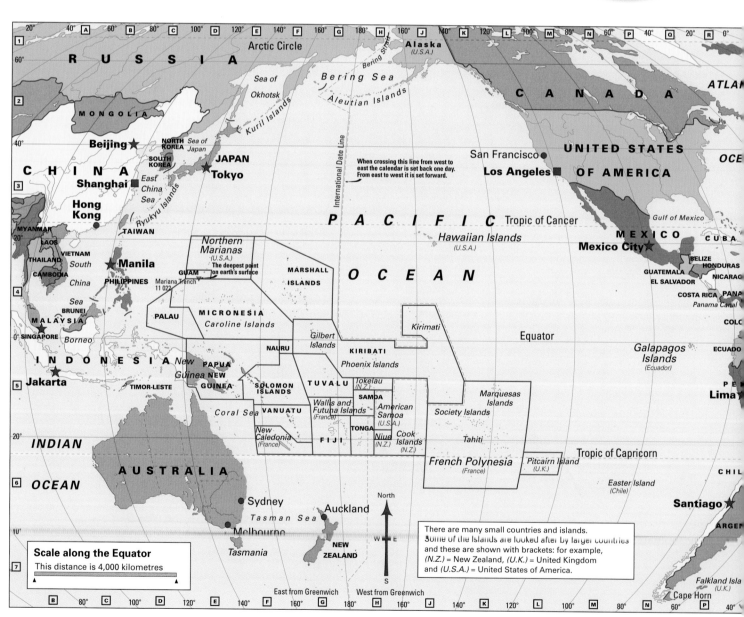

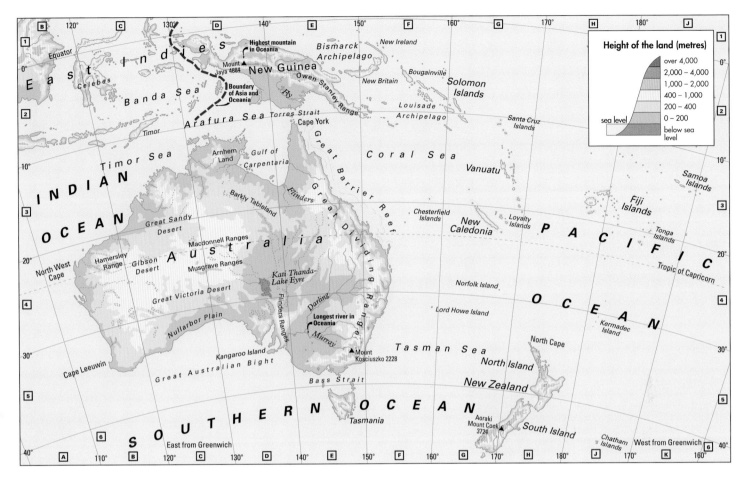

Height of the land (metres)

- over 4,000
- 2,000 – 4,000
- 1,000 – 2,000
- 400 – 1,000
- 200 – 400
- 0 – 200
- below sea level

Map 1 (physical):

Equator — East Indies — Celebes — Banda Sea — Timor — Arafura Sea — Timor Sea

Highest mountain in Oceania — Mount Jaya 4884 — New Guinea — Boundary of Asia and Oceania — Owen Stanley Range — Fly — Torres Strait — Cape York

Bismarck Archipelago — New Ireland — New Britain — Bougainville — Solomon Islands — Louisade Archipelago — Santa Cruz Islands

INDIAN OCEAN — North West Cape — Hamersley Range — Great Sandy Desert — Gibson Desert — Macdonnell Ranges — Musgrave Ranges — Great Victoria Desert — Nullarbor Plain — Cape Leeuwin — Arnhem Land — Gulf of Carpentaria — Barkly Tableland — Flinders — AUSTRALIA — Kati Thanda-Lake Eyre — Flinders Ranges — Darling — Longest river in Oceania — Murray — Mount Kosciuszko 2228 — Kangaroo Island — Great Australian Bight — Bass Strait — Tasmania

Great Barrier Reef — Great Dividing Range — Coral Sea — Chesterfield Islands — New Caledonia — Loyalty Islands — Vanuatu — Norfolk Island — Lord Howe Island — Tropic of Capricorn — Tasman Sea — North Cape — North Island — New Zealand — Aoraki Mount Cook 3724 — South Island — Chatham Islands

Samoa Islands — Fiji Islands — Tonga Islands — PACIFIC OCEAN — Kermadec Island

SOUTHERN OCEAN — East from Greenwich — West from Greenwich

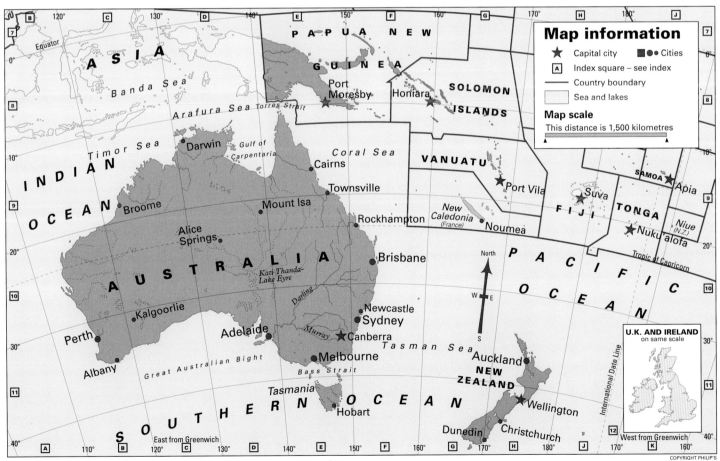

Map information

- ★ Capital city
- ■ ● ● Cities
- Ⓐ Index square – see index
- —— Country boundary
- Sea and lakes

Map scale
This distance is 1,500 kilometres

Map 2 (political):

Equator — ASIA — Banda Sea — Arafura Sea — Torres Strait

PAPUA NEW GUINEA — Port Moresby — Honiara — SOLOMON ISLANDS — VANUATU — Port Vila — Suva — FIJI — SAMOA — Apia — TONGA — Nuku'alofa — Niue (N.Z.)

INDIAN OCEAN — Timor Sea — Darwin — Broome — Gulf of Carpentaria — Cairns — Townsville — Mount Isa — Rockhampton — Coral Sea — New Caledonia (France) — Noumea

Alice Springs — AUSTRALIA — Kati Thanda-Lake Eyre — Darling — Kalgoorlie — Perth — Albany — Adelaide — Murray — Newcastle — Sydney — Canberra — Brisbane — Melbourne — Great Australian Bight — Bass Strait — Tasmania — Hobart

North — W E — S

PACIFIC OCEAN — Tropic of Capricorn — Tasman Sea — Auckland — NEW ZEALAND — Wellington — Dunedin — Christchurch — International Date Line

SOUTHERN OCEAN — East from Greenwich — West from Greenwich

U.K. AND IRELAND on same scale

COPYRIGHT PHILIP'S

North America

- North America is the third largest continent. It is half the size of Asia. It stretches almost from the Equator to the North Pole.

- Three countries – Canada, the United States and Mexico – make up most of the continent.

- Greenland, the largest island in the world, is included within North America.

- In the east there are a series of large lakes. These are called the Great Lakes. A large waterfall called Niagara Falls is between Lake Erie and Lake Ontario. The St Lawrence River connects the Great Lakes with the Atlantic Ocean.

- North and South America are joined by a narrow strip of land called the Isthmus of Panama.

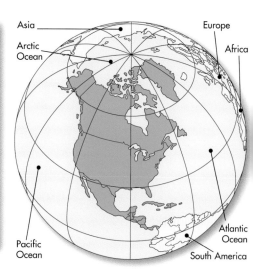

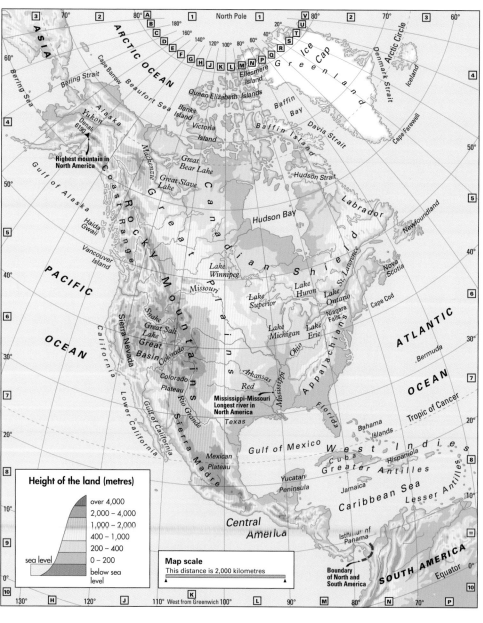

Largest countries – by area

(thousand square kilometres)

1. Canada	. . . .	9,971
2. United States	. . . .	9,629
3. Greenland	. . . .	2,176
4. Mexico	. . . .	1,958
5. Nicaragua	. . . .	130
6. Honduras	. . . .	112

Largest countries – by population

(million people)

1. United States	. . . .	335
2. Mexico	. . . .	130
3. Canada	. . . .	38
4. Guatemala	. . . .	17
5. Cuba	. . . .	11
6. Haiti	. . . .	11

Largest cities

(million people)

1. Mexico City (MEXICO)	. .	21.8
2. New York (USA)	. . . . . .	18.8
3. Los Angeles (USA)	. . . . .	12.4
4. Chicago (USA)	. . . .	8.9
5. Houston (USA)	. . . .	6.4

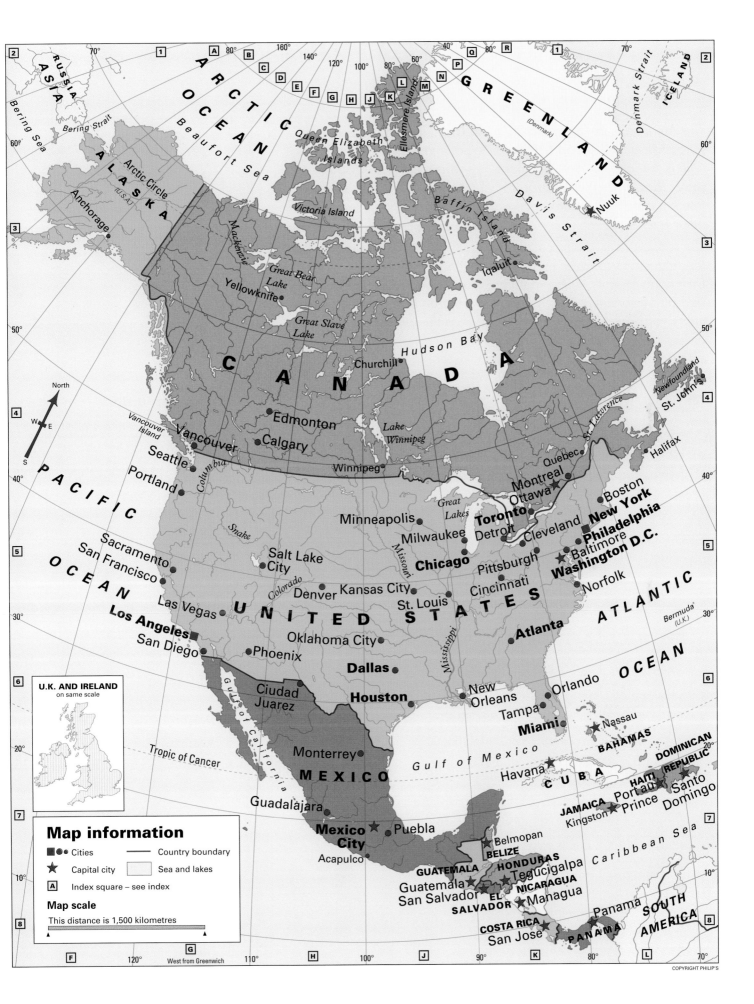

Map information

- ■●• Cities
- ★ Capital city
- Ⓐ Index square – see index

Country boundary
Sea and lakes

Map scale

This distance is 1,500 kilometres

U.K. AND IRELAND
on same scale

59

South America

- The Amazon is the second longest river in the world. The Nile is the longest river, but more water flows from the Amazon into the ocean than from any other river.

- The range of mountains called the Andes runs for over 7,500 km from north to south on the western side of the continent. There are many volcanoes in the Andes.

- Lake Titicaca is the largest lake in the continent. It has an area of 8,300 sq km and is 3,800 metres above sea level.

- Spanish and Portuguese are the principal languages spoken in South America.

- Brazil is the largest country in area and population, and has the largest city.

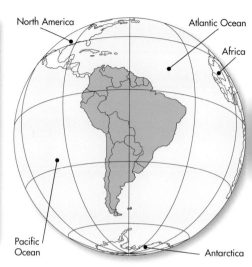

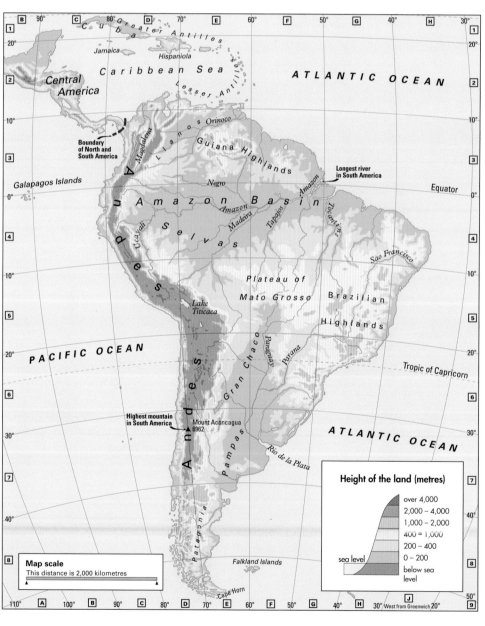

Largest countries – by area

(thousand square kilometres)

1. Brazil	. . . .	8,514
2. Argentina	. . . .	2,780
3. Peru	. . . .	1,285
4. Colombia	. . . .	1,139
5. Bolivia	. . . .	1,099
6. Venezuela	. . . .	912

Largest countries – by population

(million people)

1. Brazil	. . . .	213
2. Colombia	. . . .	50
3. Argentina	. . . .	46
4. Peru	. . . .	32
5. Venezuela	. . . .	29
6. Chile	. . . .	18

Largest cities

(million people)

1. Sao Paulo (BRAZIL)	. . . .	22.0
2. Buenos Aires (ARGENTINA)		15.2
3. Rio de Janeiro (BRAZIL)	.	13.5
4. Bogota (COLOMBIA)	. . . .	11.0
5. Lima (PERU)	. . . .	10.7

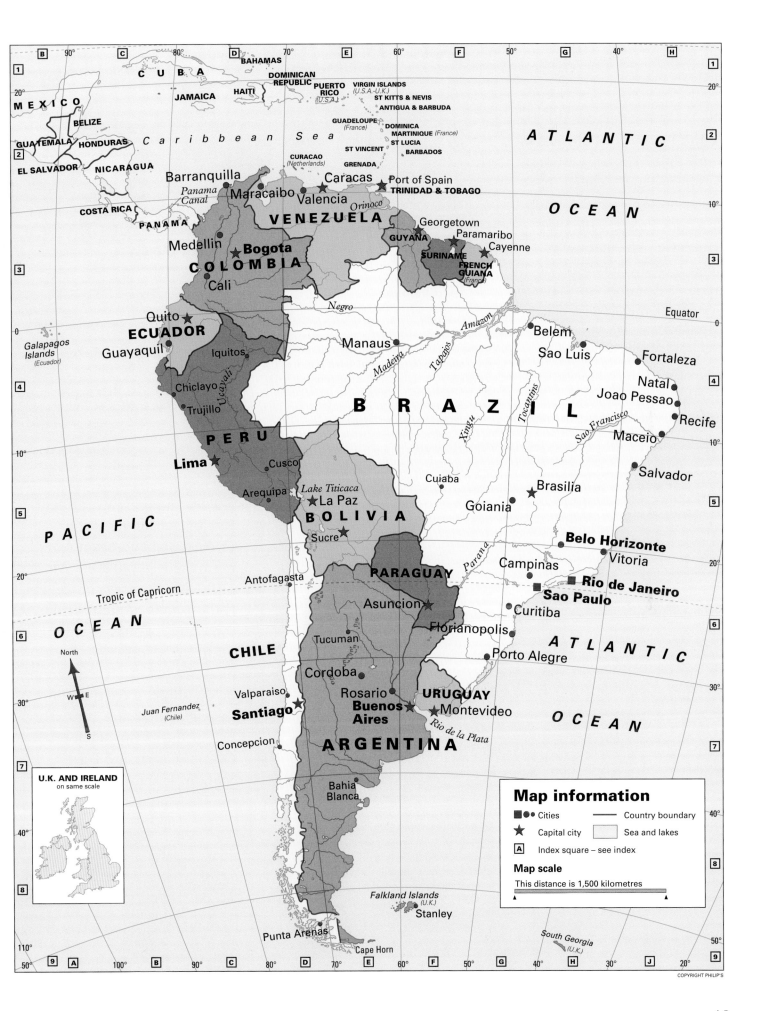

B 90° **C** 80° **D** BAHAMAS **E** 70° **F** 60° **F** **G** 50° 40° **H**

1 **1**

C U B A

20° DOMINICAN 20°

M E X I C O REPUBLIC PUERTO VIRGIN ISLANDS
JAMAICA HAITI RICO (U.S.A.-U.K.)
BELIZE (U.S.A.) ST KITTS & NEVIS

ANTIGUA & BARBUDA **2** A T L A N T I C **2**

GUA TEMALA HONDURAS *Caribbean Sea* GUADELOUPE DOMINICA
(France) MARTINIQUE (France)
EL SALVADOR NICARAGUA ST LUCIA O C E A N

CURACAO ST VINCENT BARBADOS
(Netherlands) GRENADA

Barranquilla Caracas Port of Spain 10°

COSTA RICA Maracaibo Valencia TRINIDAD & TOBAGO
Panama *Orinoco*
PANAMA *Canal* V E N E Z U E L A Georgetown
Paramaribo

Medellin GUYANA Cayenne **3** **3**

Bogota SURINAME
C O L O M B I A FRENCH
GUIANA
Cali (France)

Negro Equator
Quito *Amazon* 0°

E C U A D O R Belem

Guayaquil Manaus Sao Luis Fortaleza **4**
Iquitos
Madeira Natal
Chiclayo *Ucayali* Joao Pessao
Tapajós
Trujillo B R A Z I L Recife

Xingu *São Francisco* Maceio
P E R U *Tocantins*
Salvador 10°

Lima Cusco

Arequipa Cuiaba Brasilia **5**
Lake Titicaca La Paz
Goiania
B O L I V I A
Belo Horizonte 20°
Sucre Vitoria
Parana Campinas
Rio de Janeiro
PARAGUAY Sao Paulo
Antofagasta Curitiba **6**
Asuncion
Tropic of Capricorn Florianopolis

Tucuman A T L A N T I C
O C E A N Porto Alegre

North Cordoba
C H I L E

Valparaiso Rosario URUGUAY 30°

Santiago Buenos Montevideo **7**
Juan Fernandez Aires
(Chile) *Rio de la Plata* O C E A N

Concepcion A R G E N T I N A

Bahia
Blanca **Map information** 40°

U.K. AND IRELAND ■●● Cities —— Country boundary
on same scale
★ Capital city Sea and lakes

A Index square – see index **8**

Map scale *Falkland Islands*
(U.K.)
This distance is 1,500 kilometres
Stanley

South Georgia
(U.K.)

Punta Arenas 50°

Cape Horn

9 **A** 100° **B** 90° **C** 80° **D** 70° **E** 60° **F** 50° **G** 40° **H** 30° **J** 20° **9**

61

Polar Regions

The Polar Regions are the areas around the North Pole and the South Pole. The area around the North Pole is called the **Arctic** and the area around the South Pole is called the **Antarctic**. The sun never shines straight down on the Arctic or Antarctic so they are very cold – the coldest places on Earth. The Arctic consists of frozen water. Some parts of Northern Europe, North America and Asia are inside the Arctic Circle. A group of people called the Inuit live there.

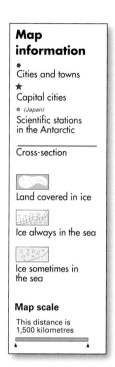

Map information

- Cities and towns
★ Capital cities
● (Japan) Scientific stations in the Antarctic

Cross-section

Land covered in ice

Ice always in the sea

Ice sometimes in the sea

Map scale

This distance is 1,500 kilometres

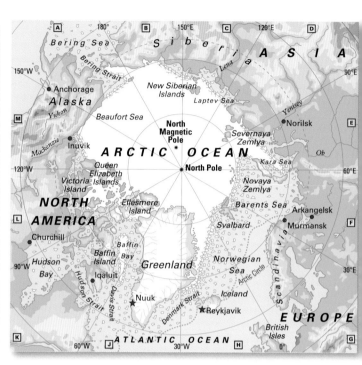

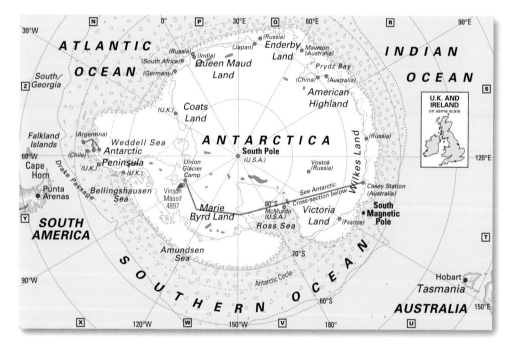

The Antarctic is a continent. It is bigger than Europe or Australia and has no permanent population. Most of the land consists of ice which is thousands of metres thick. At the edges, chunks of ice break off to make icebergs. These float out to sea. The diagram below shows a cross-section through Antarctica between two of the camps, Union Glacier Camp and Casey Station. It shows how thick the ice is on the ice sheets.

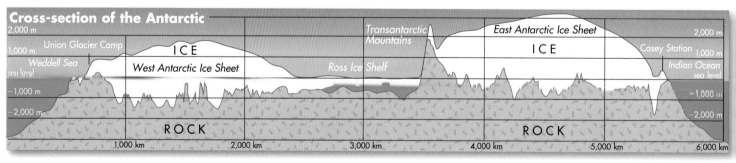

Cross-section of the Antarctic

Finding places

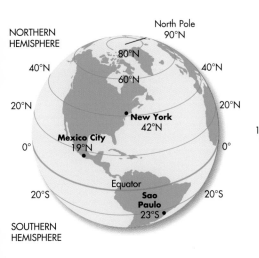

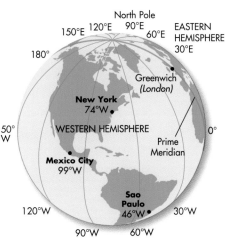

Latitude

These three maps show part of the Earth as if seen from thousands of kilometres above New York. Exactly halfway between the North and South Poles is an imaginary line called the Equator. It divides the Earth into north and south hemispheres and is numbered 0°. On either side of the Equator run parallel lines called lines of latitude.

Longitude

Maps have another set of lines running north to south linking the Poles. These lines are called lines of longitude. The line numbered 0° runs through Greenwich in London, England, and is called the Prime Meridian. The other lines of longitude are numbered up to 180° east and west of 0°. Longitude line 180° runs through the Pacific Ocean.

Map references

The latitude and longitude lines on maps form a grid. In this atlas, the grid lines are in blue, and on most maps are shown for every ten degrees. The numbers of the lines can be used to give a reference to show the location of a place on a map. The index in this atlas uses another way of finding places. It lists the rows of latitude as numbers and the columns of longitude as letters.

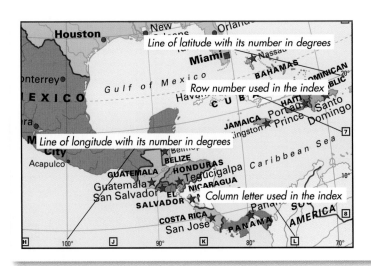

	Latitude	Longitude	Map page	Map letter-number
Cairo, Africa	30°N	31°E	55	F2
Mexico City, North America	19°N	99°W	59	H7
Moscow, Europe	55°N	37°E	51	Q4
Sao Paulo, South America	23°S	46°W	61	G6
Sydney, Oceania	34°S	151°E	57	F11
Tokyo, Asia	35°N	139°E	53	R5

This table shows the largest city in each continent with its latitude and longitude. Look for them on the maps in this atlas using the letter-number references.

Index of place names

Japan 53 R5
Japan, Sea of 53 Q4
Java 53 M9
Jedda 52 E6
Jersey 25 D8
Jerusalem 52 D5
Johannesburg 55 E8
John o'Groats 26 E1
Jordan 52 E6
Juba 55 G5
Jura 26 C4
Kabul 53 H5
Kalahari Desert 54 E8
Kaliningrad 51 L5
Kamchatka 53 S3
Kampala 55 F5
Kano 55 D4
Kansas City 59 H5
Karachi 53 H6
Katmandu 53 J6
Kazakhstan 53 G4
Kenya 55 G5
Khartoum 55 F4
Kidderminster 25 D5
Kiev 51 N5
Kigali 55 G6
Kildare 27 D3
Kilimanjaro, Mount 54 G6
Kilkenny 27 D4
Killarney 27 B4
Kilmarnock 26 D4
King's Lynn 24 G5
Kingston 59 K7
Kingston upon Hull 24 F4
Kinshasa 55 E6
Kintyre 26 C4
Kiribati 56 H5
Kirkcaldy 26 E3
Kirkwall 26 F6
Knockmealdown Mountains 27 C4
Kolkata 53 K6
Kosovo 51 M7
Kuala Lumpur 53 L8
Kuwait 52 F6
Kyle of Lochalsh 26 C2
Kyrgyzstan 53 J4
La Paz 61 E5
Labrador 58 P4
Lagos 55 D5
Lahore 53 H5
Lake District 24 C3
Lancaster 24 D3
Land's End 25 A7
Laos 53 L7
Lapland 50 M2
Larne 27 F2
Las Vegas 59 F5
Latvia 51 M4
Lebanon 52 E5
Leeds 24 E4
Leicester 25 E5
Leinster 27 D3
Lena, River 52 P2
Lerwick 26 J8
Lesotho 55 F8
Letterkenny 27 D2
Lewis 26 B1
Lhasa 53 L5
Liberia 55 B5
Libreville 55 E6
Libya 55 E3
Liffey, River 27 E3
Lilongwe 55 G7
Lima 61 C5
Limerick 27 C4
Lincoln 24 F4
Lincolnshire Wolds 24 F4
Lisbon 50 F8
Lisburn 27 E2
Lithuania 51 M4
Liverpool 24 C4
Lizard Point 25 A8
Ljubljana 51 K6
Llandudno 24 C4
Llanelli 25 B6
Lockerbie 26 E4
Lome 55 C5
Lomond, Loch 26 D3
London 25 G6
Londonderry 27 D2
Los Angeles 59 F5
Loughborough 24 E5
Lowestoft 25 H5
Luanda 55 D6
Lurgan 27 E2
Lusaka 55 F7
Luton 25 F6
Luxembourg 51 J6
Lvov 51 M6
Lyons 51 H6
Madagascar 55 H8
Madeira 55 A2
Madrid 50 G8
Maidstone 25 G6
Majorca 50 H8
Malawi 55 G7
Malaysia 53 M8
Maldives 53 H8
Male 53 J8
Mali 55 C4
Malin Head 27 D1
Mallaig 26 C3
Malta 51 K8
Man, Isle of 24 B3
Managua 59 K7
Manaus 61 E4
Manchester 24 D4
Manila 53 P7
Mansfield 24 E4
Maputo 55 G8
Margate 25 H6
Mariana Trench 56 E4
Marrakesh 55 C2
Marseille 51 J7
Marshall Islands 56 G4
Martinique 61 E2
Maseru 55 F9
Mask, Lough 27 B3
Mauritania 55 B4
Mauritius 54 J7
Mbabane 55 G8
Mecca 52 F6
Medina 52 E6
Mediterranean Sea 50 H8
Mekong, River 53 M6
Melbourne 57 E11
Merthyr Tydfil 25 C6
Mexico 59 H6
Mexico City 59 H7
Mexico, Gulf of 59 J6
Miami 59 K6
Michigan, Lake 58 L5
Micronesia 56 F4
Middlesbrough 24 E3
Milan 51 J6
Milford Haven 25 A6
Milton Keynes 25 F5
Milwaukee 59 J4
Minneapolis 59 H4
Minsk 51 N5
Mississippi, River 59 J5
Missouri, River 59 J4
Mogadishu 55 H5
Moldova 51 N6
Mombasa 55 H6
Monaco 51 J7
Monaghan 27 D2
Mongolia 53 L4
Monrovia 55 B5
Montenegro 51 L7
Montevideo 61 F7
Montreal 59 K4
Montrose 26 F3
Moray Firth 26 E2
Morecambe Bay 24 C3
Morocco 55 C2
Moscow 51 Q4
Mourne Mountains 27 E2
Mozambique 55 G8
Mull 26 C3
Mullingar 27 D3
Mumbai 53 H7
Munich 51 J6
Munster 27 B4
Muscat 52 G6
Myanmar 53 L6
Nairobi 55 G6
Namibia 55 E8
Nassau 59 L6
Natal 61 H4
Nauru 56 G5
Naypyidaw 53 L7
Ndjamena 55 E4
Neagh, Lough 27 E2
Neath 25 C6
Nenagh 27 C4
Nene, River 24 G5
Nepal 53 K6
Ness, Loch 26 D2
Netherlands 51 H5
New Caledonia 57 G10
New Guinea 57 D2
New Orleans 59 K5
New York 59 L4
New Zealand 57 G11
Newbury 25 E6
Newcastle-under-Lyme 24 D4
Newcastle-upon-Tyne 24 E2
Newfoundland 59 N4
Newhaven 25 G7
Newport 25 D6
Newquay 25 A7
Newry 27 E2
Niagara Falls 58 N5
Niamey 55 D4
Nicaragua 59 K7
Nicosia 51 P8
Niger 55 D4
Niger, River 54 D4
Nigeria 55 D4
Nile, River 54 G3
North America 30 C2
North Channel 27 F1
North Downs 25 F6
North Korea 53 P4
North Macedonia 51 M7
North Magnetic Pole 62 M
North Pole 62 E
North Sea 51 H4
North West Highlands 26 C2
North York Moors 24 E3
Northampton 25 F5
Northern Ireland 27 D2
Norway 51 J3
Norwich 24 H5
Nottingham 24 E5
Nouakchott 55 B4
Novosibirsk 53 K3
Nuneaton 25 E5
Nur-Sultan 53 H3
Nuuk 59 P2
Ob, River 52 K3
Oban 26 C3
Oceania 31 S5
Ohio, River 58 M6
Oldham 24 D4
Omagh 27 D2
Oman 52 G6
Omsk 53 J3
Ontario, Lake 58 N5
Oporto 50 E7
Orange, River 54 E8
Orinoco, River 60 E3
Orkney Islands 26 E7
Orlando 59 K6
Osaka 53 Q5
Oslo 51 J3
Ottawa 59 K4
Ouagadougou 55 C4
Ouse, River 24 E4
Outer Hebrides 26 A2
Ox Mountains 27 C2
Oxford 25 E6
Pacific Ocean 30 B4
Paisley 26 D4
Pakistan 53 H6
Palau 56 E4
Panama 59 K8
Panama Canal 61 D2
Papua New Guinea 57 E8
Paraguay 61 E6
Paramaribo 61 F3
Paris 50 G6
Pembroke 25 B6
Pennines 24 D3
Pentland Firth 26 E6
Penzance 25 A7
Persian Gulf 52 F6
Perth (Australia) 57 B11
Perth (UK) 26 E3
Peru 61 D5
Peterborough 25 F5
Peterhead 26 G2
Philadelphia 59 L4
Philippines 53 P7
Phnom Penh 53 L7
Phoenix 59 G5
Pittsburgh 59 K4
Plymouth 25 B7
Podgorica 51 L7
Poland 51 L5
Poole 25 D7
Port Moresby 57 E8
Port of Spain 61 E2
Port Talbot 25 C6
Port Vila 57 G9
Porto Alegre 61 F6
Portadown 27 E2
Port-au-Prince 59 L7
Portland Bill 25 D7
Portlaoise 27 D3
Porto-Novo 55 C5
Portsmouth 25 E7
Portugal 50 F8
Prague 51 L6
Preston 24 D4
Pretoria 55 F8
Pristina 51 M7
Puerto Rico 61 E2
Pyongyang 53 N4
Pyrenees 50 G7
Qatar 52 F6
Quebec 59 L4
Quito 61 C4
Rabat 55 C2
Rangoon 53 L7
Reading 25 E6
Recife 61 H4
Red Sea 55 G3
Ree, Lough 27 D3
Reigate 25 F6
Réunion 54 J8
Reykjavik 50 C3
Rhine, River 51 J6
Rhondda 25 C6
Rhone, River 51 J7
Ribble, River 24 D4
Riga 51 N4
Rio de Janeiro 61 G6
Riyadh 52 F6
Rocky Mountains 58 H4
Romania 51 M6
Rome 51 K7
Roscommon 27 C3
Ross Sea 62 V
Rosslare Harbour 27 E4
Rostov 51 Q6
Rotherham 24 E4
Rugby 25 E5
Russia 52 F2
Rwanda 55 F6
Sahara, desert 54 B4
Sakhalin 53 R3
Salisbury 25 E6
Salisbury Plain 25 D6
Salvador 61 H5
Samoa 57 J9
San Diego 59 F5
San Francisco 59 E5
San Jose 59 K8
San Marino 51 K7
San Salvador 59 J7
Sana 52 F7
Santiago 61 D7
Santo Domingo 59 L7
Sao Paulo 61 F6
Sao Tome & Principe 55 D5
Sarajevo 51 L7
Sardinia 51 J7
Saudi Arabia 52 F6
Scafell Pike 24 C3
Scandinavia 50 J4
Scarborough 24 F3
Scilly, Isles of 25 A8
Scotland 26 D3
Scunthorpe 24 F4
Seattle 59 F4
Senegal 55 B4
Seoul 53 P5
Serbia 51 L7
Severn, River 25 D6
Shanghai 53 P5
Shannon, River 27 C3
Sheffield 24 E4
Shenyang 53 N4
Shenzhen 53 N6
Shetland Islands 26 J8
Shrewsbury 24 D5
Siberia 52 J2
Sierra Leone 55 B5
Singapore 53 L8
Skopje 51 M7
Skye 26 B2
Slieve Donard 27 E2
Sligo 27 C2
Slough 25 F6
Slovak Republic 51 L6
Slovenia 51 K6
Snaefell 24 B3
Snowdon 24 B4
Sofia 51 M7
Solihull 25 E5
Solomon Islands 57 G8
Somalia 55 H5
South Africa 55 F8
South America 30 F5
South China Sea 53 M8
South Downs 25 F7
South Korea 53 P5
South Magnetic Pole 62 T
South Pole 62 S
South Sudan 55 F5
Southampton 25 E7
Southend 25 G6
Southern Ocean 31 K7
Southern Uplands 26 D4
Southport 24 C4
Spain 50 F7
Spey, River 26 E2
Sri Lanka 53 K8
St Albans 25 F6
St Andrews 26 F3
St David's Head 25 A6
St George's Channel 27 E5
St Helens 24 D4
St Kitts & Nevis 61 E2
St Louis 59 J5
St Lucia 61 E2
St Petersburg 51 P4
St Vincent 61 E2
Stafford 24 D5
Stansted Airport 25 G6
Start Point 25 C7
Stevenage 25 F6
Stirling 26 E3
Stockholm 51 K4
Stockport 24 D4
Stockton 24 E3
Stoke on Trent 24 D4
Stonehenge 25 E6
Stornoway 26 B1
Strabane 27 D2
Stranraer 26 C4
Stratford-upon-Avon 25 E5
Sucre 61 E5
Sudan 55 F4
Suez Canal 55 G2
Sumatra 52 M9
Sunderland 24 E3
Superior, Lake 58 L5
Suriname 61 F3
Suva 57 H9
Swansea 25 C6
Sweden 51 K4
Swindon 25 E6
Switzerland 51 J6
Sydney 57 F11
Syria 52 E5
Tahiti 56 J5
Taipei 53 P6
Taiwan 53 P6
Tajikistan 53 H5
Tallinn 51 N4
Tampa 59 K6
Tanganyika, Lake 54 G6
Tanzania 55 G6
Tashkent 53 H4
Tasmania 57 D12
Taunton 25 C6
Tay, River 26 E3
Tbilisi 52 F4
Tees, River 24 E3
Tegucigalpa 59 K7
Tehran 52 G5
Telford 24 D5
Thailand 53 L7
Thames, River 25 G6
The Hague 51 J5
Thimphu 53 L6
Thurso 26 E1
Tianjin 53 N5
Tibet, Plateau of 52 K5
Tigris, River 52 F5
Timbuktu 55 C4
Timor-Leste 53 P9
Tipperary 27 C4
Tirane 51 M7
Titicaca, Lake 60 E5
Togo 55 D5
Tokyo 53 R5
Tonga 57 J9
Toronto 59 K4
Torquay 25 C7
Tralee 27 B4
Trent, River 24 F4
Trinidad & Tobago 61 E2
Tripoli 55 E2
Tunis 55 D2
Tunisia 55 D2
Turin 51 J7
Turkey 52 D5
Turkmenistan 52 G5
Tuvalu 56 G5
Tweed, River 26 F4
Tyne, River 24 E3
Tynemouth 24 E2
Uganda 55 G5
Ukraine 51 M6
Ulan Bator 53 M4
Ullapool 26 C2
Ulster 27 D2
United Arab Emirates 52 F6
United Kingdom 50 G4
United States 59 G5
Ural Mountains 50 V2
Uruguay 61 F7
Urumqi 53 K4
Uzbekistan 53 G4
Valletta 51 K8
Vancouver 59 F3
Vanuatu 57 F9
Venezuela 61 D3
Verde, Cape 54 B4
Victoria Falls 54 F7
Victoria, Lake 54 G6
Vienna 51 K6
Vientiane 53 M7
Vietnam 53 M7
Vilnius 51 N5
Virgin Islands 61 E2
Vistula, River 51 L5
Vladivostock 53 P4
Volga, River 51 S6
Volgograd 51 R6
Vyrnwy, Llyn 24 C5
Wales 25 C5
Walsall 25 E5
Warrington 24 D4
Warsaw 51 L5
Wash, The 24 G5
Washington D.C. 59 L5
Waterford 27 D4
Watford 25 F6
Wellington 57 H12
West Bromwich 25 D5
West Indies 58 M7
Western Sahara 55 B3
Westhill 26 F2
Weston-super-Mare 25 D6
Westport 27 B3
Wexford 27 E4
Weymouth 25 D7
Wick 26 E1
Wicklow 27 F4
Wicklow Mountains 27 E4
Wight, Isle of 25 E7
Winchester 25 E6
Windhoek 55 E8
Winnipeg 59 H4
Woking 25 F6
Wolverhampton 25 D5
Worcester 25 D5
Worthing 25 F7
Wrath, Cape 26 C1
Wuhan 53 N6
Wye, River 25 C5
Yamoussoukro 55 B5
Yangtse, River 53 M5
Yaounde 55 E5
Yekaterinburg 51 T4
Yellow Sea 53 P5
Yemen 52 F7
Yenisey, River 52 K2
Yerevan 52 E4
York 24 E4
Yorkshire Wolds 24 F4
Zagreb 51 L6
Zagros Mountains 52 F5
Zambezi, River 54 G7
Zambia 55 F7
Zimbabwe 55 F7